247301

D1196833

CONTRARIES

CONTRARIES

A Personal Progression

Stuart Holroyd

THE BODLEY HEAD
LONDON SYDNEY
TORONTO

© Stuart Holroyd 1975
ISBN 0 370 10445 5
Printed and bound in Great Britain for
The Bodley Head Ltd
9 Bow Street, London WC2E 7AL
by Redwood Burn Limited,
Trowbridge & Esher
Set in Monotype Imprint
by Gloucester Typesetting Co. Ltd
First published in Great Britain 1975

For Sue

*'Without contraries is
no progression.'*
William Blake

CONTRARIES

I

One of the things that most irritated me about Carol after I had fallen out of love with her was that she seemed to attract misfortune. Things just didn't go right for her. She was always having her money stolen or losing her bloody little Peke, or getting the curse on the very day when she had to go for a crucial audition. I had an idea in those days that unlucky people always brought their misfortune on themselves, that if they were unloved by the gods they deserved nothing better. It was one's duty to put oneself so in tune with the life forces that there was no question of ever being unlucky. It took me some time to find out that Carol was one of life's unfortunates, nor could I have remotely conceived when we first met that I was to be her biggest misfortune ever.

Her mother had died some months before and she had been looking after her father, who was a doctor in the country. She wanted to be an actress, to go to London and take the theatre by storm. Finally her father took on a housekeeper and let her go. She rented a room in the Notting Hill area, near us, and happened to meet my friend, Bill Hopkins, who brought her round to the house one afternoon. She was twenty-two and had been in London for three weeks. She was thrilled out of her mind to fall in with a bunch of geniuses, not only self-styled but publicly acclaimed.

I had a secret theory at that time that I had a certain advantage over my friends where women were concerned. Women, I thought, don't go for compulsive talkers. They may confide in them and establish good friendships, but they don't go to bed with them. They prefer someone more soulful and deep, someone who gives the impression of having mysterious areas that are irreducible to mere words. I not only gave the impression, but I really had such areas. At least, I very much wanted to undergo the shattering experience of a love affair, with the emphasis on *love*.

I was twenty-four and had behind me a broken marriage, some dozen affairs and two published books which had earned me a reputation as a prodigy sprung miraculously from the lump of the working class. This was in the late 1950s when you had to be plebeian, impoverished, arrogant, angry, self-educated and earnest to be the darling of the publishers and the press. I was. I remember the headline on the front page of the *Evening News* the day Anne was granted her decree nisi: 'Stuart Holroyd Divorced.' That made me feel I had really arrived.

Yes, there was a hell of a lot of vanity and arrogance in us, and one can well understand the about-turn of the critics, the press and the publishers after we'd been over-exposed for a couple of years. We were upstarts and freebooters, tied neither by property nor parental responsibilities. And we were obviously having a lot of fun and a lot of sex, which are not the acknowledged perquisites of fame. 'Immature', 'irresponsible', 'coffee-bar Messiahs', 'living in cloud-cuckoo land', 'on cloud nine', 'only just started Shavian', 'all my I': these were some of the remarks with which the propertied, the privileged and those stuck in the parental-pedagogic syndrome attempted to put us down. I don't say they were not deserved, but they were damned uncharitable and niggardly.

Despite my affairs, and a four-year marriage which had been founded on sex and cemented by poverty, I felt that in all these relationships there had been an important element missing. And I had taken to heart the remark, which many people had made, that I'd never be a great writer until I was capable of love. (Others had prescribed 'suffering', but I didn't know what that was or how to go about experiencing it.)

I suppose Carol was ripe for a love affair too, at twenty-two and after her sheltered life. When we'd broken up I told myself that there had been about our affair·from the start something theatrical, that we'd been hamming it a bit, acting like great lovers, kidding ourselves and each other. But now, at fifteen years' distance, I see it differently. I think both of us wanted from life at that time an experience that went deep, that gave us a sense of really living rather than skimming the surface of life, and that the wish was strong enough to create the illusion.

She seemed extraordinarily beautiful to me. She had long dark hair and large brown animated eyes, good features, a serious turn of mind, and ambition. There was nothing wary or knowing about her. She was so unlike other girls who had been around London for some time.

I was even rash enough to confess to Bill that I was in love, which produced a characteristic reproof:

'An absurd and undignified condition. It results in impairment of judgment, loss of drive, criminal squandering of time and energy. To be in love is to confess to being a mediocrity.'

There was never anything tentative about Bill, and he was never at a loss for words or an opinion. He was Welsh, from a theatrical background, and in conversation was dramatic, entertaining, eloquent and combative. He chain-smoked thin hand-rolled cigarettes, was usually unshaven and tousle-haired and had a kind of ravaged look which went well with his wild genius image but was probably produced by malnutrition, sleeplessness and excessive smoking. He had written some fine poetry in his teens, had had a very successful career as a journalist in his early twenties, from which he had retired to become a novelist and propagandist. He was my closest friend at the time, and secretly I both envied him for his articulateness and extroversion and scorned him for his unflagging hilarity and overdeveloped sense of the dramatic.

Bill, Tom Greenwell and I had a shabby terrace house in Notting Hill, and there was a spare room which Colin Wilson and John Braine shared the rent of in order to have a *pied à terre* in town. The social centre of the house was Tom Greenwell's room. Tom was unique among us in that he had no pretensions to genius. He had a genius, however, for friendships, and he would dispense to all comers, at all times of day and night, tea, wine when he could afford it, and conversation, which he regarded as an art. He was a newspaper gossip-columnist and served as our hot line to Fleet Street, and he wrote for his own amusement sharp little satires in rhymed couplets. The door of his room bore the notice: 'Beware of the Doggerel.' He was thirty-six and had thinning hair, cadaverous cheeks, a long nose and large ears: a combination of features that often got him tagged as 'Mephistophelian'. He knew *Omar Khayyam* and a lot of eighteenth-century literature by heart, and he affected dandyish waistcoats and a long cigarette-holder.

He too had a characteristic *bon mot* re my infatuation with Carol.

'Love is the wisdom of the fool and the folly of the wise,' he proclaimed with a flourish. When Bill congratulated him on his aphorism he confessed that he'd borrowed it from 'my dear friend Sam Johnson'.

But neither Tom's mockery nor Bill's admonition cut any ice with me. I was in love and they, mere men of words, could waste their breath on each other.

Covering an entire wall of my room was a montage of press cuttings, letters and photographs. I remember worrying about whether I should take down the nudes before taking Carol there for the first time, but I decided not to. Perhaps the place ought to be cleaned up a bit though, I thought. One lives with one's smells and doesn't notice them, but to a visitor the room would probably reek of dust, old socks, rotting vegetables and cooking. Also, there was dust under the chairs and the table and on the floorboards where the ragged carpets came to an end. The long windows that looked out onto Chepstow Road were caked with grime, and the bottoms of the curtains were tattered. The place would probably seem dingy and squalid to a doctor's daughter just up from the country, but on the other hand she might go for the *vie de Bohème* atmosphere. So I left everything exactly as it was, even the waste-bin piled high with tea-leaves, potato-peelings and eggshells.

'Oh, what a *marvellous* idea,' Carol enthused, when she saw the wall montage. 'It must be a mirror of your personality.'

'It's my filing cabinet,' I said.

I had bought some cheap Spanish wine for the occasion. We sat on the floor in front of the gas-fire, leaned back against the couch and sipped the wine, and Carol talked about herself, about life with father, and about her mother's death. The fire hissed and gave off a red glow and I listened and watched the expressions that flitted across her face, and the lights in her hair.

'Am I boring you?'

'No, I'm interested. I'm interested in everything about you,' I said.

'It's difficult to believe that someone's dead,' she said, still talking about her mother, 'to think that there's nothing at all left of all the fun that was in them and all their odd ways. Then it suddenly strikes you that you're never going to see them again. I remember washing some of her clothes in the sink about three weeks after she'd died, and I suddenly realised that it was *her* dirt that I was washing out of the clothes, that she had worn these next to her skin and that the dirt that swilled down the drain was now all that was left of her. I couldn't bear to rinse the rest off the side of the sink. I just broke down in shuddering tears. Can you imagine it?'

'I can, very well,' I said, and took her hand, and Carol was grateful and adoring, and when we made love it wasn't a seduction but literally a consummation, and afterwards she said:

'Oh, they're so wrong, those people who say it's underrated. It's the most marvellous experience I've ever had. But I always knew it would be, with the right man.'

'It was for me too,' I said, which was what she wanted to hear, though it wasn't entirely true. I had employed all my acquired finesse to give her pleasure, but all my own pleasure had been in heightening hers and I had remained detached throughout, the virtuoso giving a skilful performance. That wasn't the way I had meant or expected it to be. It was bewildering and a little galling to find the joys of true love were not more poignant and mind-shattering.

'I'm so happy, and so frightened,' she said.

'What of?'

'Of it ending. It's bound to one day, isn't it?'

'Not necessarily,' I said, but I wished that I could sound more convincing and convinced.

In the semi-darkness Mr Gilbert, the Peke, nosed over my waste-bin and found a lamb chop bone which he began gnawing noisily.

Of course everyone in the house soon knew. A gentleman doesn't kiss and tell, they say, but such is male vanity and pride in conquest that I doubt that even an impeccable gentleman would be above the sly innuendo. Anyway, I was no gentleman and Carol was in love and perhaps a bit proud too, so everyone soon knew.

To my surprise, Bill disapproved. I couldn't put it down to jealousy, for it was axiomatic among us that jealousy was an emotion unworthy of the man of genius. Colin Wilson and I had at one time quite amiably shared a mistress, and I had even shared my wife for a time with another friend, Michael Hastings, who subsequently married her.

'Carol's an innocent,' Bill said. 'She's a sensitive, spiritual girl. You shouldn't corrupt her.'

I said I knew and that was what I valued in her and that I wouldn't dream of corrupting her, and Bill gave me one of his theatrical quizzical looks and emitted a loud burst of laughter. He laughed too, later, when he found me reading *The Life of St Teresa*. He knew that Carol was reading it and accused me of pretending to be interested in her mental and spiritual life when all I cared about was getting her to bed. I denied it, but couldn't convince him. Bill believed in, and professed to have, mental and spiritual relationships with women, but he firmly believed that they were incompatible with sexual involvement.

'Spiritual' was the word we all made very free with. If anything made us cohere as a group, Bill, Colin and I, it was a shared conception of man as a creature with spiritual hunger, a dynamic evolutionary drive. We held that mystical experiences, visionary states of consciousness, moments of ecstasy, of joy, of world-and-life-affirmation, were not only relevant to life but should be the chief object of man's endeavour. 'Religious existentialists' we called ourselves. 'Spiritual fascists' we were called by our critics. The time was not very hospitable to unsectarian religious thinking. Official philosophy in the universities was dominated by the logical positivists, whose horror of metaphysical statements was hysterically spinsterish, and the prevailing intellectual orthodoxy was that of the New Left, whose preoccupations were political and social. To both groups, 'spiritual' was a dirty word, which was partly why we tended to use it as a rallying call. Or, rather, Bill and Colin did. I felt I had enough rallying to do in myself, to establish some consistency between my life and my ideas. Bill was wrong. I fully appreciated Carol's qualities, and hoped to find in her a woman worthy of spiritual and intellectual love and capable of taming my unregenerate urge to sexual conquest.

One of Bill's schemes at this time was a plan to take over a small theatre on Westbourne Grove. It had been empty for some time, and Bill had approached the owners, 'on behalf of a syndicate of well-known writers', to negotiate a lease. 'We need a writers' theatre,' Bill argued. 'The directors, actors, technicians are the little men, the minions. The writer is the creative element in the theatre, and it is a fundamental principle of creation that the artist must have full control of his medium. And I mean literally *full* control of every detail, from over-all policy down to the price of seats and the decision whether to serve coffee in the interval. That's what I mean by a writer's theatre.'

Thus Bill, as quoted in Tom's newspaper column. One of the national dailies picked up the story the following day, and when we went round to see the theatre, Bill, Tom, Carol and I, we were accompanied by several journalists and someone from television.

The place reeked of must and damp and a wan grey light filtered thinly through grimy windows high in the walls. Some of the rows of seats were overturned and the carpeting in the aisles was worn and full of holes. The place had the smell and look of a dead building awaiting the demolishers.

But Bill was not daunted. He paced the stage and announced, 'This place is going to be the nerve-centre of a theatrical revolution. It will be what the Royal Court was under Granville-Barker.'

'Granville-Barker had Shaw,' one of the journalists called out from the auditorium.

'We have a dozen Shaws,' Bill countered pugnaciously. 'And don't get me wrong. I think Shaw was the greatest dramatist of this century—so far. The potential of the Shavian theatre has yet to be exploited. Nobody took up where he left off. Shaw's theatre was the theatre of intellect. And what have we had since?—the drawing-room and the kitchen sink! It's time for a revolution in the theatre, and this is where it will begin.'

Tom, mounting the steps to the stage, said, 'All Shaw's plays were operas,' but no one took up this point.

The journalist asked, 'And where's the money coming from?'

'We have powerful allies,' Bill said darkly.

His enthusiasm was irresistible. I stood on the stage and envisaged the auditorium packed with people applauding my latest production. I had worked in a repertory company for a year after leaving school and had a play produced by a university dramatic society, and was nostalgic for all the fuss and hurry, the noise and the sense of occasion that make the life of the playwright so rewarding compared with the lives of writers who labour in solitude to produce books for anonymous readers.

'Isn't it exciting?' Carol was standing beside me, gazing out into the auditorium. 'I can just see it. Can't you?'

I could see the dark fire-opals of her eyes, the radiance of her face, the tense excitement that possessed her whole body. 'Yes, I can just see you holding the stage like a Bernhardt or a Duse, playing the audience like an instrument,' I said.

Carol said, 'I wonder what the dressing-rooms are like? Of course you high and mighty writers don't care a damn what kind of squalor the humble actor has to live in.'

'Let's go and look,' I said.

The dressing-rooms were indeed squalid. The wash-basins and mirrors had a patina of dust and grease, the armchairs and couches looked as if they had been savaged by vandals.

'You see!' Carol said with an air of triumph.

I had eyes only for her. I kissed her, and the excitement was enhanced by the dirt and dinginess, the lure of greasepaint, memories of the days when I'd worked in the theatre, and visions of the triumphs we would share, as author and actress, in the future.

We were actually quite poor at this time, though all the publicity probably gave people the impression that we were coining small fortunes. Colin had done quite well with *The Outsider*, but my books hadn't done much more than cover the advance royalties that my publisher had paid on acceptance, and my main source of income was £5 a week in advance on future royalties, which I collected from Gollancz's office in Covent Garden every Friday. I managed to supplement this with odd earnings from journalism and television, but I had to watch every penny and save shillings for the omnivorous gas-meter. Bill was equally penurious, and before Carol came along we tended to live on a diet of eggs, chips, sausages, bread and tea, with an occasional five-shilling meal at a restaurant in Notting Hill. An unforeseen bonus of my affair with Carol was that she turned out to be a marvellously inventive and economical cook. She would come round in the late afternoon or early evening and cook a meal for us all, and we would stay up talking and drinking tea, and sometimes I would walk her home, but more often she stayed and we went to bed. It wasn't long before her having a place of her own began to seem an unnecessary expense and I started to entertain thoughts of having her move in with me.

We seemed in those first weeks marvellously compatible. The theatre project gave us a lot to talk and dream about and plan, but it wasn't only in our ambitions that we established links. We explored each other's loneliness, and with the avidity of lovers for total possession we talked about our past lives. I had never thought mine particularly interesting, especially compared with that of Colin, who from his early teens had been making definitive choices, experiencing existential crises, and suffering and creating like mad. For me, life had only really begun when I moved down to London at the age of eighteen. But Carol probed beyond that. She wanted to know everything, and she was so easily amused and so readily moved to sympathy that I found myself telling her things that I had almost forgotten because they had seemed irrelevant.

I told her about my modest start in the theatre, and how at the age of fourteen I had attached myself to a summer show which used to come to Blackpool every year. It offered an unsophisticated, even crude form of entertainment to the seaside holiday crowds, but to me it represented a glamorous world of colour, freedom and opportunity. I was a day-boy at a direct-grant public school to which I had won a scholarship at the age of eleven, and a powerless rebel against the system which sought to turn out officers, gentlemen and graduates of the more august universities. For me the theatre represented what today would be called the 'alternative society', and theatre people were glamorous because, being themselves rootless and egotistical, they had no tedious counsels about what I should do with my life.

Today there's a lot of sympathy for kids who kick against the system, but the generation that my parents belonged to, that had suffered the privations, sacrifices and tragedies of the war years in defence of the values of freedom and opportunity, neither understood nor sympathised with kids who ungratefully rejected the boons of Mr Butler's Education Act and Mr Attlee's Welfare State. I was bright enough to pass my 'A' levels and get accepted for a university place, and my parents were horrified when I opted for what I called the 'University of Life'. I wrote a letter to the manager of the resident repertory company in Blackpool recommending myself as a young actor and writer of exceptional promise, and got the producer of the summer show to sign it. Weeks later I received a reply offering me a job as assistant stage manager at £3 a week.

I was overjoyed. I had chosen a career. I had rejected the way prepared and laid out for me by parents and teachers and had embarked on a way of life in which the future was unpredictable and a challenge.

The trouble was, I was the world's worst actor. I was too withdrawn and introspective to be able to project myself into a part. By the time I told Carol about it, I could look back on my year in the theatre with humour, but at the time it had been one long experience of humiliation. I had turned up on the first Monday dressed in my best suit, and had immediately been set to work making an awning out of wood and dirty canvas for a 'Riviera set' that was required for that evening's new play. After twelve hours' continuous work on that first day I went home exhausted and with some of my illusions about life and about the theatre severely shaken. Life was so much more hectic, mundane and businesslike than it had been in the summer show, and the people were different too, altogether more sober, reserved and hard-working. Their attitude seemed to allow me no other identity than that conferred by my position as A.S.M., and as A.S.M. I was at everyone's service, for fetching beer from the pub around the corner on Saturday nights between shows, as well as for keeping the cast supplied with the props that they would require on stage. I was not a person, I was a function, a cog in the machine that worked ceaselessly to stage a different play every week. I was resentful and humiliated, and I was not only a deplorable actor but an incompetent A.S.M. as well. I failed to put essential props on stage, neglected to give the signal to bring the curtain down on a very dramatic act ending, and was always losing my place in the prompt copy because I was reading poetry instead. I fell so far into disfavour with the company that the only way I thought I could redeem myself was by writing them a masterpiece. So I wrote a play about Thomas Chatterton, the brilliant boy poet of Bristol who was driven by the world's neglect and incomprehension to commit suicide at the age of eighteen. I gave a copy of my play to the producer and one to the manager of the company, and waited in suspense for weeks to be acclaimed the boy genius of Blackpool. But it didn't happen. The producer said the play was 'promising but a bit too wordy' and the manager said hypocritically that he didn't think they would be able to give it the production it deserved. So I packed up the theatre and went to London.

London in the autumn of 1952 was a city recovering from war. It was scarred and dingy and there were still extensive bomb sites. Rubble, greyness, smog, poverty, garish whores on the streets in Soho, trams still running along Kingsway, tramps sleeping on the Embankment and under the Arches: it was a run-down city by today's standards, but for me it was romantic and exciting and just what I had expected from my reading of Dickens.

I found an attic room in Pimlico for thirty shillings a week. It was rather like the room Chatterton had died in according to Henry Wallis's painting: small, with the ceiling sloping in on two sides, and with a little window overlooking the rooftops. The furniture comprised the bare necessities: a bed, an upright chair and a tattered old armchair, a washstand, a small table, a chest of drawers There was also a gas-fire and a gas-ring, the latter to be used, a notice on the wall stated, only for boiling and not for frying because of the fire risk. The landlady, however, was a kindly disposed woman who had had sons of her own, and she let me use her gas-cooker in the basement whenever I wanted to fry some bacon, sausages or chops.

Food was still rationed, and you had to produce a little brown book for the butcher or grocer to clip coupons out of whenever you bought anything. This didn't really affect me because I had to make stringent economies anyway. My only income was the dole, supplemented by National Assistance, which produced just over £3 a week. Twice a week I walked to the Westminster employment exchange in Horseferry Road and 'signed on' as an out-of-work actor. The rest of the time I spent very agreeably, reading, writing, visiting art galleries, exploring London.

On one of my exploratory walks I came to Portman Square and saw an impressive corner building with a brass plaque announcing 'The Poetry Society' beside the door. I went in and introduced myself as a poet and critic, and received from an old lady, the secretary, and a really venerable-looking gentleman, the librarian, the warmest of welcomes. The old gentleman was talking about Swinburne and Rossetti, whom he had known personally, but he had no time for the moderns. The library, however, was well stocked with poetry and dramatic literature of all ages, and when I learnt that I could use it at any time I didn't hesitate to produce a guinea as my subscription to the Society. It proved to be money well invested, for I not only had the use of their central-heated library during the winter months to study and write in, but I actually earned money from them by writing articles for their quarterly, the *Poetry Review*. The venerable librarian who had welcomed me so warmly came to regard me as a pernicious infiltrator, for I wrote articles on T. S. Eliot, Dylan Thomas, and even a German called Rainer Maria Rilke.

My first weeks in London had been lonely but my passion for poetry soon gained me friends. Following up an advertisement in the *New Statesman* I got in with a group of young men and women who met every Sunday night in a room above a pub in Westminster to read poetry to each other. They would take it in turns each week to expound a theme illustrated by readings. I chose for one of mine 'The Poetic Expression of Religious Experience', and in researching for it I came upon the theme for my first book. Poetry, I argued, is not just 'the right words in the right order' or the expression of prettily-turned sentiments about nature or about life, it is an instrument for exploring reality and the self. The theme certainly provoked argument.

When the pub closed at ten we used to continue our arguments in the Strand Corner House, which was open all night. The hard core of the poetry-reading group consisted of young men in various underpaid jobs who lived close to the poverty line in cold inhospitable bed-sitters, and they stayed together not only for earnest talk about life and art, but also for warmth and companionship. The winter of 1953 was very cold, and gas-fires were expensive, so all sorts of people who were down on their luck thronged public libraries, station waiting-rooms, cheap cafés, churches, and places where warmth could be had for nothing or at the most for the price of a cup of tea. I reckoned myself lucky to have the Poetry Society library almost to myself, and I kept my find a secret from my poetry-loving acquaintances in the Strand Corner House.

It was there that I met Alfred Reynolds. I remember the occasion vividly. It was a night when smog had reduced visibility to about ten feet, which made the journey from the pub to the Corner House quite an adventure. London was eerily silent under its pall, and the statues in Parliament Square and along Whitehall loomed suddenly out of the mist like avenging angels. The poetry-lovers made their way in high spirits, laughing and chasing each other, hiding in doorways and behind monuments, keeping in touch with calls and whistles, all oblivious of death in the noxious air. But Alfred was older and wiser. He made his way to the Corner House as quickly as he could with a muffler wrapped round his mouth, and was already sipping tea when we arrived.

It was the first time Alfred had attended one of the poetry readings. I had noticed him there, a man in his mid-forties, heavily built, who spoke with a soft foreign accent. When I mentioned Rilke in the discussion that followed the reading, he said that it was good to find an Englishman who read foreign poets, even though he himself found Rilke a bit too romantic and mystical. I argued heatedly that Rilke was a great poet because he was a visionary who had succeeded in communicating his vision by creating a private imagery and mythology. Alfred countered that to retire into a private world was no answer to the problems confronting modern man. I replied that Rilke hadn't retired into a private world but on the contrary had cultivated the faculty to take the outer, contingent world into himself and transform it. Alfred said that was mysticism. We went on for well over an hour, and the others either got bored and left or started up conversations of their own. Before we parted that night, Alfred gave me his address and invited me to a meeting at his house the following Tuesday.

The house was one of a long row of small, suburban 'semis' situated in the anonymous urban wasteland somewhere north of Cricklewood. Alfred clearly enjoyed being incognito. He worked by day as a civil servant and was proud that none of his colleagues remotely guessed that off duty he was outspokenly critical of the system that they all unquestioningly accepted and lived under. He was Hungarian, had come to England in the 1930s, and had been employed by British Intelligence during the war to 'de-Nazify' German prisoners. He had done so very successfully, employing the Socratic method of leading a man by gentle questions and promptings to contradict or condemn himself out of his own mouth. As a result, he had found himself after the war with a following of young German converts eager to practise his methods and propagate his philosophy. The philosophy was, inevitably in a man of his generation, chiefly political, and consisted mainly in the rejection of all ideologies and the championship of the freedom of the individual. Alfred saw enemies of the individual everywhere. Politicians, leaders of business, the Churches, people involved in television, in advertising, were all conspiring to produce a world in which freedom in action or even in thought would be impossible. They must be resisted by individuals all over the world meeting together, talking over problems, freeing each other from illusions and conditioned modes of thought. Collectively such individuals might be referred to as 'the Bridge', for they not only sought to bridge the gap between people of different nationalities, creeds and ideologies, but also comprised a bridge from the present pretty deplorable state of the world to a more hopeful future.

I had never been very interested in politics, but the rejection of authority, the emphasis on the freedom of the individual, and also perhaps the implied elitism of the 'Bridge' philosophy appealed to me. I became a regular at the Tuesday evening meetings in Alfred's house, where I was able to enjoy not only stimulating conversation but also tasty continental food (Alfred was a great mixer and blender) and music. The evening always began with music. Alfred had a large collection of 78s. Beethoven, Mahler and Bruckner were his favourite composers. I fell under the spell for a time of the brooding, soulful and whimsical mid-European artistic temperament. Alfred presented me with a slim volume of poems which he had published in Budapest in 1931, and I accepted it with due gratitude for the honour, though of course I couldn't read a word of Hungarian. But what I chiefly gained from Alfred was an introduction to new literary experiences. The 'Bridge' discussions were full of references to Kafka, Mann, Koestler, Hesse, Orwell, Nietzsche, and above all Dostoevski, whose 'Legend of the Grand Inquisitor' was something of a scripture for the 'Bridge' philosophers. I felt my education deplorably lacking, and I read and read to make up for it. For months my brain reeled with questions of freedom and destiny, sin and guilt, good and evil, justice, God, death. It was all new and exciting, and I read and thought and talked avidly, until Alfred came to regard me as his most prominent lieutenant and even hinted that there would come a day when I would be ready to set up on my own as a teacher of the 'Bridge' philosophy.

How often must fantasies of power and influence have been entertained in garrets in Pimlico, Islington, Fulham, Hampstead!

I felt sure that I was destined for great achievements, but at the same time I was painfully aware that my work to date was pitifully incommensurate with my dreams. During my first months in London I sold three short stories to magazines, two literary articles to the *Poetry Review* and two or three pieces to *The Stage*. At the same time I read Kafka, Dostoevski, Lawrence, and wished to God that I might have a vision or an obsession that would lift me out of the rut of workaday scribblers. Just round the corner from my lodgings was a house with a blue plaque announcing that Aubrey Beardsley had once lived there. I would have sold my soul to know that, one day, a similar plaque would bear my name. I was nineteen and I couldn't see how adult life could be supportable without fame. Through my reading, I had lived on more intimate terms with the mighty dead than with any of my undistinguished contemporaries, and I felt sure that there must be a place for me in the pantheon. Of course, I would have to win it, but I was not averse to work, to sacrifice, to suffering. In fact, I wished I could suffer more, as Dostoevski, Kafka, Lawrence had done. It wasn't enough to be poor and living in a garret, particularly when one hadn't been forced into the position by relentless circumstances but had chosen it for oneself.

In one particular, however, I suffered quite acutely. My fantasies were not all of power, fame, influence, blue plaques and the world's acclaim. I had erotic fantasies too. Nothing extravagant though. This was 1952 and post-war stringency and rationing extended to the market in sex fantasies. Young men weaned from puberty on *Lilliput* and *Men Only* with their coy pin-ups, and perhaps if they were lucky an occasional ogle over *La Vie Parisienne*, didn't have much to go on when it came to fantasising about sex. I had a little more to go on than most, for during my last year at school and the year I worked in the theatre I had had a 'regular' girl-friend, Anne, with whose co-operation I had at least been able to explore the peripheries of the intriguing territory of sex. Anne starred in my erotic fantasies, and supporting roles were played by girls seen on tube-trains or buses or in art galleries. I once ventured to speak to a girl in an art gallery and even got her to go to the theatre with me to see Donald Wolfit in *Volpone* at Hammersmith, but I was too inexperienced in effecting a smooth transition from cultural to carnal communication, and when I tried to seduce her I did so

gauchely and received a sharp rebuff. I spent some evenings walking the streets of Soho looking at the incredible women who would
sell themselves for a pound or two, but they were gaudy and
raucous and offered, I knew instinctively, not a fulfilment of fantasies, but only disappointment, shame and self-disgust. My letters
to Anne became more romantic and passionate, and eventually in
spite of her parents' opposition she joined me in London. She was
just eighteen. Anne, too, fell under the spell of Alfred's middle-
European charm. We went together to the Tuesday evening meetings and Anne eagerly read the prescribed books and learnt to talk
as passionately as any of us about philosophical anarchism, freedom, the dignity and sacredness of human life and the evil of
ideologies. She took a job as a typist, and as we could then afford
an extra pound a week for rent we moved into a larger room in
Belsize Park. We began to talk about marriage. It was clearly unnecessary for two enlightened people who believed in freedom and
the dignity of life to enter into a legal contract which could only be
regarded as based on mistrust and a craven desire for security, but
on the other hand marriage would make life easier in various little
ways and would reconcile us to our parents, who might even come
up with some substantial token of their relief at their children's
conversion to the paths of righteousness. So, on a clear, crisp day
in February 1953 we were married at the register office on Haver-
stock Hill. Alfred was best man and our parents came down from
Blackpool for the occasion, my mother bringing with her a wedding
cake which she had baked some two months before in shrewd
anticipation of the occasion.

Four years later we were separated and I swore I'd never marry
again. Life, I believed, must be conceived and lived as a quest, a
process of continual growth, and for two people whose paths happened to cross and who found they had profound affinities at a
particular juncture of time to shackle themselves together for fifty
years seemed not only foolish but life-denying.

But 'Say you love me', said Carol after the first time we went to
bed together, and 'Will you always?', and I gave her the answers
she wanted because she was trusting and vulnerable. Well, how do
you make love without invoking eternity? I mean make love, not
one-night lays. When an affair goes on for some time, one of you
is going to come up with the eternity bit sooner or later. In our

case, it was Carol, and on the first occasion. But I wanted a *love* affair. So I assured her that love wasn't necessarily short-lived, though I wasn't convinced of the fact myself. However, I cared for her too much to be able to lie cynically to her. To lie cynically is to lie and know you're doing so and not give a damn. I lied quite uncynically, for I convinced myself as well. During the first weeks of the affair with Carol I thought and talked a lot above love. There had to be some way out of the problem of having to pretend it was eternal in order to persuade a woman it was real.

The fact that we considered ourselves rather exceptional people was a help. And the spiritual bit. I argued that a true understanding of love does not conceive it as something that is 'mine', but as something of which one can be the expression. Love, I said, is a process of giving out which is endless and inexhaustible because what is being given out is not coming from one but through one. 'Oh yes,' said Carol, thinking of acting and inspiration and the divine spark. And she agreed when I said that love is not a finite and personal thing, but is infinite and of God. It follows, I argued, that we should not regard love as a commitment willingly entered into, but as a revelation of the primal committedness of our being to the world through a particular person who focuses it. Her assent to this was less enthusiastic, but she allowed for the fact that I had something of a reputation as a philosopher and was inclined to talk in this way. And as we were exceptional people, like Shaw and Ellen Terry, she had to agree that jealousy and possessiveness, which proceeded from the 'my love' way of thinking, were unworthy emotions.

So far so good, but what about sex?

'I couldn't bear the thought of your doing that to someone else,' Carol said one night after we'd made love.

'I don't want to,' I said, and it was quite true. We were enjoying a vigorous and wholly satisfying sex life. 'It works so well for us,' I said, 'because we've brought sex and love together. Believe me, it doesn't often happen. In fact, it's never happened to me before. Sex in itself is a drive that seeks only its own gratification. It's the root cause of the "my love" way of thinking. It's not infinite and of God. What we have to do and what I think you and I have done, is regard sex as a function of love and not the other way round. If we do that, there can be no question of possessiveness or jealousy.'

A palpable *non sequitur*. But if Carol saw through the speciousness of the argument, she didn't say so. I think that perhaps a touch of *folie de grandeur* had jammed up her feminine intuitions. We were, after all, the great writer and the great actress, and so our love had to be something unique, spiritual and impassioned, not selfish, possessive, muddled and human like that of lesser beings.

So there was no question of marriage, though we did have something of a honeymoon. It was in Cornwall, at the expense of the National Film Board of Canada. They were going to Cornwall to interview Colin Wilson and wanted Bill and me to go too. I said I'd only go if Carol could come with us, and Carol said she couldn't go without taking her dog. So early one autumn morning we all set off from Notting Hill crammed into a van and a car: six film men with all their equipment, Bill, myself, Carol and the dog. The producer was a burly Canadian who talked at length and graphically about breaking in horses, and who wanted to stop for a 'noggin' every fifty miles. The journey took nearly fifteen hours, but the beer was free, and it was fun to be going to Cornwall to harangue the Canadians and to be able to take one's mistress on expenses.

The actual filming wasn't much fun, though. Colin was interviewed in the comfort of his home, but the Canadians weren't going to traipse all the way down to Cornwall without getting a bit of local colour for the folks back home, so Bill and I had to be portrayed as peripatetics, striding along beaches and cliffs engaged in earnest discussion.

They chose Pentewan Bay for the main film sequence. This is a sandy bay about a mile wide which in summer is packed with caravans and tents. A stream running down from the clay-pits around St Austell turns the sea white for about a quarter of a mile out. Here, one bleak November morning in 1958, we went to make history. A bitter wind was cutting in from the sea and up the valley. Bill, Carol and I sat in the car with the heater on while the technicians set up their equipment. Mr Gilbert scampered around stupidly in pursuit of seagulls, then yapped to be let into the car and jumped all over us with wet sandy paws and underbelly. Within seconds the warm air in the car was fetid with the pungent smell of dog. I was glad when the producer signalled that they were ready for us.

But they weren't. They kept us standing round for five or ten minutes while someone attended to the power supply. I said I thought it was all a waste of time and we ought to be at home getting on with the job of writing.

'This'll be a historic documentary,' said Bill, rolling a thin cigarette with shaking fingers. 'Surely that's worth suffering a little discomfort for?'

'I don't see why history has to be made in this God-forsaken place,' I said. 'It could just as well be done in the bar of the Fountain.'

'Too cosy,' said Bill. 'The great writer today has to be an ascetic.'

The producer instructed us to walk towards the camera in conversation and to stop about ten feet away, where the recording equipment could pick up our voices. To make it look natural, Bill could stop to light his cigarette at that point. That reminded me of an occasion in my brief inglorious career as an actor, when I, a non-smoker, had had to light a cigarette on stage. The cigarette had stuck to my lip make-up and when I tried to remove it my fingers had slipped along to the lighted end and I had exclaimed involuntarily at the pain. Another dramatic moment ruined. It was the story of my life as an actor.

We followed the producer's directions, strolled up to within ten feet of the camera and paused for Bill to light his cigarette. The wind blew out the three matches but he managed it with the fourth.

'When you think of it, Stuart,' he said conversationally, 'the literature of the last ten years in this country has been distinguished only by its total lack of imagination and drive. There hasn't been one monumental character created, not a single new idea propounded. Between the wars we had Yeats, Eliot, Joyce, Lawrence. What have we had since? A generation of literary pygmies.'

'Yes,' I agreed, 'the generation that came out of the war seemed to have been spiritually deadened by the experience. They'd lost their nerve. Whereas in France . . .'

'Cut there!' said the producer, stepping forward in front of the camera. 'I'm sorry, but we're having trouble with the sound. The wind doesn't help. You'll have to come a bit closer. And, Stuart, try and look a bit more natural, less wooden, you know. Perhaps it'd help if you lit a cigarette too.'

'I don't smoke.'

'No, of course. Well, just try and forget the camera. We'll take it again from the beginning.'

We walked away from the camera and then, on a signal from the producer, back towards it. Bill lit his cigarette and began, 'When you think of it, Stuart, the literature of the last ten years in this country . . .'

'Cut!' They were still having trouble with the sound. The producer apologised and went to confer with the sound technician in the back of the van. He called out that there would be a ten-minute break.

Mr Gilbert had given up seagull-chasing and settled down to smell quietly on the back seat. Carol took my hands and rubbed them vigorously when I got into the car beside her.

'Incompetent fools!' Bill exploded. 'How do they expect us to have a coherent conversation if they're going to interrupt it every other minute?'

'I don't know that I can be coherent anyway,' I said. 'It's un-natural, standing out in the middle of Pentewan Bay in a gale shouting at each other about modern literature. The Canadians'll think we're nuts.'

'Or fanatics,' Bill said. 'That's all right. That's the image we want to create. But we must plan what we're going to say. Obvi-ously under these conditions it's got to be pithy and to the point. What were you going to say about France when they cut us short?'

'Just that existentialism emerged out of the Resistance, out of the experience of men in extreme situations.'

'For whom questions of freedom betrayal, solitude and death weren't merely academic, but were daily realities. Good. That's the stuff. But we don't want to give Sartre and Camus too much publicity. This is a programme about English writers.'

'Who by comparison have been narrow and parochial, pre-occupied with subjects of class. . . .'

'And personal relationships.'

'Yes, and have cultivated the qualities of sensitivity and charm at the expense of energy and imagination.'

'Good. Great stuff. And we'll go on to talk about the need to create heroes. The writer today must dare to be great and to tackle great themes.'

'Right. And to do that he needs to have a sense of crisis. Greatness is a response to a challenge, an extreme situation.'

'How about throwing in a reference to Elvis Presley or the James Dean cult,' Bill said, 'just to show that they're symptoms of a crisis in our civilisation? The kids are frightened and lost, and they react by looking for hero figures and leaders.'

I nodded. 'A good point.'

We spent another hour and a half, intermittently stopping and starting up again, and at the end of it the producer said, 'We should be able to edit five or six minutes of usable material out of that.'

'Do you wonder that most film stars are neurotic idiots?' Bill said.

'Come on, I'll buy you a noggin,' said the Canadian.

We had arranged to meet Colin after the morning's filming for a drink at the Fountain, a pub near the quay in Mevagissey. He was already there when we arrived, in the middle of a group of people whom a tourist might have taken for local fishermen. Most of them had weathered or bearded faces and wore duffle coats and thick roll-neck jerseys of coarse wool. Some were refugees from uncongenial jobs or broken marriages, others writers or artists who had no success and probably had no talent but whom obstinate dedication or fear of change, or sheer laziness, kept reconciled to a life of poverty and hardship. Today they would be called 'drop-outs', a more neutral and even sympathetic term than those current for the type in the fifties, when they were known unequivocally as misfits, no-goods, dead-beats or failures. They were thick on the ground in Cornish seaside villages, where life was cheap in winter and there was a living to be gleaned in one way or another from the tourist trade in summer. Though the type was often maligned, they constituted collectively the subsoil from which the artistic and intellectual life of the fifties drew its nourishment. They were opinionated and often naive, anti-authority in all its forms, anti-royalty, anti-police, anti-cultural humbug of the mandarin school, anti-America, anti-war, anti-hanging, anti-big-business. True, their rejections were too sweeping and smacked of the sour grapes of the under-privileged, but they constituted a challenge to the conscience of the age that in the decade that followed produced a revolution in popular music, more official recognition of the rights and needs of minorities, and even some

31

legislation. They were, on the whole, serious, articulate, quick to establish friendships, and good with children, and though they were inclined to be pessimistic they at least thought and cared about the kind of world their children would grow up in and have to cope with. As they set little value upon property or money, they had few inhibitions about making use of what others had gained by hard work or good luck. Colin Wilson was popular with the Mevagissey group because he always kept their glasses full and was often good for a touch. He would never let anyone buy him a drink in return. His generosity was legendary, but it was also, I thought, ambiguous. There was less in it of convivial benevolence or indifference to money than of old-fashioned lordly magnanimity and unwillingness to put himself under the slightest obligation to anyone.

His manner was not the least lordly, however. He would assert of other writers that they were fools or mediocrities and claim that he was the greatest living English writer, but he was not at all condescending. He enjoyed and indeed told the odd dirty joke, and he would listen to other people's opinions and involve himself in their problems or experiences. In a group such as had gathered at the Fountain that morning he was conspicuous only in that he was cleaner shaven and looked younger than most of them. He was wearing a thick blue fisherman's jersey and baggy brown trousers. He retained something of the look of the school 'swot': high brow, thin mouth, small eyes behind thick glasses, short back and sides haircut; and when he moved or shook hands he did so jerkily, as one not quite at ease with his body. He was quite tall and broadly built, but no one would ever take him for a sportsman of any kind.

Nor was Bill at all interested in sport, though he had become quite keen on darts lately. He had a theory that a man of strong enough will could exercise power over inanimate objects and he played darts with intense concentration and determination. As soon as we got into the Fountain he challenged the Canadian producer to a game. The producer cheerfully accepted, and bought a round of drinks first. Carol and I sat at a table, where Colin presently joined us.

'How did it go, Stuart?'

'It was bloody cold, and they say they only got six or seven minutes of usable material out of it.'

'That's quite a bit of film time. Enough to make an impression. You know, Stuart, I'm convinced it's vital that we get ourselves better known on the other side of the Atlantic. I've already made a breakthrough there; *The Outsider* is selling well and I'm going out there to do a lecture tour next year.'

'That's great,' I said, 'but I don't think Houghton Mifflin have even sold out the first impression of *Emergence from Chaos*, and to judge from the reviews there won't be any demand for a second.'

Colin nodded thoughtfully. 'Of course, you and Bill have suffered from the backwash of my publicity. Those bastards the critics got embarrassed because on second thoughts they reckoned they'd praised me too extravagently, so when your books came out they savaged them.'

'Well, you had advertised us as the only other two geniuses in England,' I pointed out.

'Why not? It's true. The buggers were just too mean-spirited to admit it. Still, they'll come round. We just have to keep producing work and ignore them. What are you working on now?'

'A play,' I said. I reached across the table and took Carol's hand. Colin, I thought, had pointedly ignored her. I was faintly annoyed.

'Good,' Colin said. 'But you should get down to another serious philosophical book. We've got to put English existentialism on the map. Sartre is basically too pessimistic, too low-key. Husserl's important. His concept of "intentionality" is central to the new existentialism. Look, why don't you come and put in a solid stint of work down here? Get another book done. You can have the chalet to yourself and have meals with us.'

That proposal, too, pointedly ignored Carol. 'I'll think about it,' I said.

'For some reason, he hates me,' Carol said when we were preparing to go to bed in our hotel room that evening. It was a small room cheaply furnished, heated by an ancient one-bar electric fire and lit by a central hanging light-bulb with no shade. The paintwork was dark green and the walls were covered with a mottled brown wallpaper against which hung three tawdry paintings depicting harbour scenes. The room did nothing to alleviate a feeling of depression that had been building up in me all day. We had spent the afternoon watching the filming of the interview with Colin at his house and the evening drinking at the Fountain. The day had somehow sapped my energies. I had found prolonged conviviality and playing the role of the celebrity curiously enervating, and what I wanted most from Carol was tranquillity, warmth and love.

'He doesn't hate you,' I said a little tetchily. 'I admit he's been rather cool towards you, but he is with everybody until he gets to know them well.'

'Cool, you call it! It was as if he was trying his best to make me feel superfluous.'

'I know,' I said, 'but take no notice. You're not superfluous. You know that. I need you. Come to bed now. It's been a very wearing day. I want to relax, with you in my arms.'

Bless her for being so easily conciliated, I thought, when she came to bed.

Colin had said, that evening, when we had found ourselves side by side in the Gents at the Fountain, 'I don't know why it is, Stuart, but she gives me the willies.'

I had wanted to say, 'You're speaking of the woman I love,' but I hadn't been able to do it, even self-mockingly. I had answered tamely, 'She's an intelligent and understanding girl and I'm very fond of her.'

It had been a kind of betrayal and had contributed to my feeling of depression.

She fell asleep first, lay soft and trusting in my arms. Dear innocent Carol, girl gifted with passion and compassion, doctor's daughter from Essex, would-be Bernhardt, a good woman fallen among geniuses.

Colin had made enough money from *The Outsider* to buy a house. He had originally gone to Cornwall to get out of the lime-light and reorientate himself. He had no longer been able to work in London. In three months he had become, to his own and his friends' amazement, something of a national figure. 'At twenty-four, with his first book, Mr Wilson steps straight into the front ranks of major writers,' one of the papers had trumpeted. He was inundated with offers from publishers, newspapers, magazines, theatres, television programmes, hostesses. His book sold some 50,000 copies in three months, and his name became known to millions. The publicity was not all favourable, for he represented different things to different people. To his admirers he was the working-class hero who had fought his way to the top. They made much of the fact that he had left school at sixteen, worked as a laundryman, a hospital porter, a table-clearer in a Lyons Corner House, had lived rough in Paris and London, sleeping out on Hampstead Heath at night and working in the British Museum reading-room during the day. To the academics his success was symptomatic of the erosion of the standards of sound scholarship. Professor Ayer, reviewing his book, quoted Dr Johnson's quip about a woman's preaching being like a dog's walking on his hind legs: 'It is not done well; but you are surprised to find it done at all.' Literary people were on the whole more generously disposed, and conceded his vitality, breadth of reading and originality of theme, but some deplored the inelegance of his style, and Arthur Koestler dismissed *The Outsider* as the work of 'a young man who has just discovered that genius is prone to Weltschmerz'. Both the extraordinary success of the book and the ambivalence of people's reception of it were probably attributable to the fact that it was the kind of book that many people felt they could have written if they had thought of it first. Colin took the acclaim as his due and the criticisms as the drivel of fools. It was the notoriety that he was unprepared for. His opinions on numerous topics were eagerly canvassed by journalists and television interviewers, and he, like many a young man before and since who has suddenly found himself listened to, enjoyed being outrageous and shocking. He was always good 'copy' and inevitably the media men probed further into his background and private life. They dredged up the fact that he had had a child by and had married a woman ten years older than himself, had left them some three years before and was now living with a woman to whom he wasn't married. To the image of the cocky and opinionated young genius was added that of the callous and unprincipled lecher. It was distressing not only for him but also for the parents of Joy, the girl he was living with. One evening her father went round to their flat and demanded that she return home with him and never see Colin again. There was even talk of horsewhipping. At the time of the intrusion they had some guests, one of whom must have tipped off the newspapers, for it was all over the front pages the next morning. The story was embellished with a real horsewhip and served up as a symbolic drama, a confrontation between the old order and the new, the righteous anger of the gentleman of principle and the effrontery and cynicism of the upstart. Cartoonists had a field day. It was too much. Colin and Joy fled to Ireland with journalists in hot pursuit. When it had all blown over Colin gave up his London flat and moved into a rented cottage in Cornwall. When he was talked about in London, it wasn't uncommon to hear the terms 'come-uppance' and 'nine days' wonder' associated with his name. But *The Outsider* kept selling, came out in America and in numerous translations, and Colin kept writing and produced another two books, both of which got a bad critical reception but nevertheless went into several impressions. After eighteen months in the cottage he decided to settle in Cornwall and bought a larger house.

It was not a step a so-called 'Angry Young Man' could take without some examination of the issues of conscience involved. Though Colin was no rabid socialist, he was certainly acquainted with Proudhon's dictum that 'Property is theft', and he had the bohemian's contempt for bourgeois values and pride in being independent and unfettered. However, his accountant had persuaded him that he had a choice between putting his money into a house or into the coffers of the tax man. There was no old-world charm about the house he bought, though, nothing suggestive of his having adopted the role of the cultivated man of letters. It was a post-war brick and pebble-dash structure, uncompromisingly functional inside and out, set on a hillside overlooking the sea and with two acres of long grass around it. There were shelves of books and records in every room, representing a considerable cash outlay, but the furniture was cheap and ordinary and the interior decoration and lighting were undistinguished and haphazard. Everything about the place declared that although Colin had become a man of property nobody was going to be able to accuse him of being a man of taste.

On the last day the Canadians wanted to film an interview with Colin, Bill and me together in Colin's work-room. This was a room at the bottom of the house, reached down a steep flight of steps from the kitchen or through a door from the adjacent garage. It had large windows on two sides and all the wall space was covered with bookshelves. Colin did his work seated in a deep armchair with his typewriter on a swivel table that he drew across in front of him. At the beginning of the filming he pushed it aside as if he was interrupting his work for the interview. Bill and I were sitting opposite him on collapsible beach chairs which he had brought in from the garage. Colin taped the interview on a portable tape-recorder. The interviewer, a man about Bill's age in a green cord jacket and colourful shirt and tie, sat between us.

'Colin, would you tell us something about how you three came together?' he began. 'I believe you knew each other before any of your work was published?'

'Yes,' said Colin, settling into his chair and looking directly at the camera, 'I first met Bill in Paris in 1952. He was working as Press representative of the Campaign for World Government, and I was trying to make a living by selling subscriptions to the *Paris Review*. We met at someone's flat. I remember the occasion well. Bill was arguing the case for world government so vigorously and persuasively that I thought, "Here's a man of genius who's misdirecting his talents." I told him as much, said he ought to be writing. He said he was, and when he showed me some of his stuff, poems and short stories, I was delighted to find that it had qualities that I was beginning to think were non-existent in English writers of my generation. I immediately recognised an ally.'

'What qualities?' said the interviewer. 'Could you expand on that a bit?'

'Yes, well, put briefly I would say precision, hardness, economy and imaginative realism. I felt very strongly that English writing had become flabby and self-indulgent, lacking muscle.'

'Is that how you felt, Bill?' the interviewer asked.

'Yes, exactly.' Bill nodded vigorously.

'And Stuart Holroyd, how about you? Did you know Colin and Bill at this time?'

'No,' I said, 'I didn't meet Colin until early in 1954.'

'And did you immediately recognise an ally?'

There was a hint of sarcasm in the way he asked it, which didn't escape me.

'Well, I didn't think in terms of alliances at the time,' I answered. 'But in Colin I recognised a writer I had affinities with.'

'It seems strange, doesn't it, that you should all have met before any of your books were published, and that you all made your mark within a year?'

37

The implication there was that Bill and I had jumped on Colin's bandwagon.

'Not really,' Colin said. 'There's always a tendency for the best minds of a generation to seek each other out quite early on. Think of Coleridge and Wordsworth, Russell and Whitehead, Pound, Yeats and Eliot.'

'And how exactly did you and Stuart meet?'

'Through a fellow called Alfred Reynolds who ran a discussion group in Dollis Hill. It was called "the Bridge" and propagated a kind of humanist, rationalist, gentle anarchist philosophy. Both the philosophy and the group seemed to me wishy-washy, and I told them as much, said they were asking all the wrong questions. So I was banned from the meetings. But they also held what they called "cultural evenings", at which they listened to music and read bits from the poets and philosophers to each other. I got the idea of presenting my indictment of "the Bridge" in terms of an anthology. I got Stuart to help me initially because he was a good reader. But it turned out that he'd been getting increasingly dissatisfied with Reynolds and his ideas, and he joined me enthusiastically in putting the anthology together. When the evening came, we had great fun demolishing "the Bridge" philosophy and shocking Alfred's followers out of their tidy little minds.' Colin chuckled gleefully at the memory.

'And this was, what, two years before you published *The Outsider*?'

'Yes, after that Stuart and I met often and talked about our ideas and started pacing one another on critical books.'

'And then presumably you brought Stuart and Bill together?'

'That's right. Bill got started on his novel, and it was a race between us to see who would get published first.'

'And now that you're all published and successful authors, does this process continue? I mean, the pacing each other on books and cross-fertilisation and discussion of works in progress? Bill?'

'Yes, certainly it does,' Bill said. 'I think it's very important that writers should stand together. People are going to pay that much more attention when three or four writers are saying the same sort of thing.'

'And what sort of thing are you saying? Collectively, I mean.'.
The interviewer smiled, clearly pleased with the way he'd turned

it. 'I'd very much like to have an answer from each of you to that. What would you say, Stuart?'

Whatever one said was going to seem naive and inadequate. Still, one had to have the courage of one's convictions and take up the challenge.

'It's a big question to give a short answer to,' I said, 'but just off the cuff I'd say that what we're all three agreed on is that the values, the attitudes and the traditions of liberal humanism are not relevant to the world we're living in today. They collapse into pessimism and defeatism when they come up against the terrible and irrational forces at work in our world. We need to develop a new religious attitude.'

'Thank you. Bill?'

'I agree entirely,' Bill said. 'I'd just add that as writers we need to evolve a new conception of the heroic. And by that I don't just mean reverse the present tendency to write novels around so-called anti-heroes. The implications reach beyond literature. The hero is the man who dares to break new ground, to disregard rules and precedents and strike out on his own. He may be an artist, a scientist, a philosopher, a politician. The important thing is that he has vision, he dares, and he isn't afraid of the responsibilities of leadership.'

'Thank you, Bill. Now, Colin, have you anything to add to that?'

'Yes, first let me say that I endorse both Bill's and Stuart's statements. What they both come down to is that the survival of our civilisation depends on its evolving a higher type of man. The crucial question is: how? I'd argue that we must take a scientific approach to the problem. We need a phenomenology of human evolution.'

'Well, thank you Colin Wilson, Bill Hopkins, Stuart Holroyd,' the interviewer said, nodding to each of us in turn. 'We won't take up any more of your valuable time. You all obviously have your work cut out.'

So he ended, getting in his snide last word. Colin and Bill, however, seemed pleased with the way the interview had gone, and so was the producer, who insisted on celebrating the conclusion of the filming with a noggin at the Fountain.

The houses in Chepstow Road have been cleaned and smartened up now and no doubt have changed hands at four or five times the amount they could have been bought for in the late fifties. Then the authentic bohemian life was still possible, for one could live cheaply. The writers who lived in our house paid thirty shillings a week each for their rooms, though this was cheap even for those days, for their rents were subsidised by the girls who occupied rooms in the basement and on the ground floor, where they pursued a profession clearly more lucrative than writing, since two of them ran MG sports cars on it. The landlord was a cheery cockney called Les, aged about forty, who turned up with his blonde, plump, overdressed wife about once a month to collect the rents. He followed the careers of his literary tenants in the papers with great interest, and I wondered whether his leniency over the rents was a form of patronage or a shrewd way of ensuring a respectable cover for the profitable activities in the lower part of the house.

Whatever Les earned from his property, he ploughed none of it back. On the exterior of the building the stucco was flaking away, and the inside was dingy and shabby. The hall, stairs and landing were all brown and dirty white, and the stairs were laid with green linoleum. There was a bathroom on the first half-landing with a sliding door of frosted glass. The bath was served by an ancient rusty gas geyser, which for a shilling in the meter would produce enough hot water for a bath, though it made alarming explosive and roaring noises in doing so. My room was on the first floor, overlooking Chepstow Road. On the same floor, at the back of the house, was the spare room which Colin Wilson and John Braine shared. Bill had the corresponding room on the second floor as a work-room, and the one above mine belonged, as the warning on the door announced, to the demon doggerel poet, Tom Greenwell. A narrow staircase lined with bookshelves that Bill had put up led from the second floor to the attic, which was Bill's bedroom. Every room had gas and electricity meters, and on the second half-landing there was a tap projecting from the wall with a shallow triangular sink fitted into the corner below it. Apart from the bathroom, this was the only water supply in the whole house. Tom said the place had 'all modern inconveniences'.

Of all the rooms, Tom's had the most lived-in appearance. The furniture was the nondescript junk of bed-sitters, but around it Tom had contrived an atmosphere of studied decadence. Tacked to the wall above his divan bed was an Arabian carpet with an embroidered harem scene. On the other walls were two large prints, one of Burne Jones's 'King Cophetua and the Beggar Maid' and the other, called 'The Penitent', depicting a naked girl kneeling before an altar, with a group of severe-robed nuns looking on. Slotted in all round the mirror above the mantelpiece were invitations, postcards and photographs of friends, many of them strikingly attractive women. On a hook beside the fireplace hung a mask of the Devil, with florid cheeks, little horns, bushy eyebrows and drooping moustache. 'My Doppelganger,' Tom called it, though for all his affected decadence and diabolism no one had ever known him to be other than courteous, generous and sympathetic. On his desk there was a small Olympia portable typewriter and a square cut-glass decanter which an elaborately engraved silver label announced was for 'Crusted Port'. The room was always warm, for from the moment the first autumnal chill was felt Tom kept an oil fire going day and night, which produced not only warmth but also a pervasive smell of paraffin fumes. He sometimes lit joss-sticks to counteract the smell, and when he had one burning and had his red bedside lamp on the atmosphere of decadence was complete.

The house generally, and Tom's room particularly, drew visitors like a magnet. It was not only the association with people and events currently in the news—though this was undoubtedly part of its appeal—but also a sense of its being a haven of disorder, a place where there were no set times for anything, where life's normal primary concerns, with eating, sleeping, earning a living, took second place, and primacy was given to conversation, creative work, friendship and the organisation and execution of grand designs. Life began about midday and went on until three, four or even five o'clock the following morning. People called in at all times of the day and night and could be fairly confident of a welcome in one or other of the rooms. There were fellow writers and journalists, people in publishing or television, and a host of seekers, malcontents and misfits who found the conversation and the atmosphere of the place stimulating. Bill and I tended to regard it as part of our duty as leaders of our generation to be accessible to all who might need us, an attitude which brought into our orbit a number of cranks and people with psychological problems. Our therapy consisted of exhortation and advice, based on the view that Freudian psychology was misconceived and that it was not sexual frustration but frustration of the creative urge and of the need to perceive meaning and direction in life that was the root cause of modern man's ills. We had different 'bedside manners'—Bill's the more hortatory and severe, mine analytical and sympathetic—and we solemnly recommended to each other 'cases' that we felt would benefit more from the other's approach. Tom would have no part in any of this, for he professed himself lacking in the necessary certainties and altruism, but his room became the social centre of the house because he was warmer, less demanding and more genuinely hospitable.

The key to the charm of this particular *vie de bohème* was its spontaneity. If someone suggested going out for a meal, to a party or to see a particular film or show, or roaming round the junk shops around Portobello Road, or taking advantage of the availability of a car to drive out to see Shaw's house at Ayot St Lawrence, others would fall in with the plan and an enthusiastic little group would be formed for the venture. Droppers-in and hangers-on never quite knew what they might get involved in. 'But when do any of you work?' some of them asked in awe. My answer was that I liked to write between about eleven o'clock at night and four in the morning, though in fact I often spent several of these hours talking in Tom's room, for Tom returned from his evening's gossip-foraging and 'putting the paper to bed' shortly after midnight. Bill worked more spasmodically, at odd times of the day and night for an hour or two, or in two- or three-day spurts, when he went off to his mother's house in South London and was incommunicado. He made out that writing was for him a tremendous travail, a matter of grappling with his 'angel', and indeed when he returned from his South London trips he often looked worn out, though he never showed anyone what he had written and I often wondered whether his 'angel' might not be flesh and blood.

Early one evening not long after our return from Cornwall, I was with Bill and Tom in Tom's room and I took the opportunity to tell them of a plan I had formulated.

Bill's reaction was predictable. 'What! Bring Carol to live here!' he said. 'It's madness, sheer madness. You're a writer. You need solitude. Besides, you should know by now that all relationships based on sex are short-lived.'

'This one isn't based on sex,' I said. 'Sex is just a part of it.'

Bill smiled as if to call my bluff. 'Anyway, no writer should be tied to one woman,' he said. 'You need variety, you need material, you need the satisfaction of conquest. Most great men are prodigious womanisers.'

'Prodigious bastards,' Tom put in. He was standing in front of his wardrobe mirror struggling with a starched shirt-front and bow-tie as he had to cover a charity ball at the Dorchester that night.

Bill ignored him. 'Just think, Stuart,' he went on, 'in a few months or perhaps weeks you'll meet someone else you'll want to take to bed. And where will you take her if you're living with Carol?'

I shook my head and smiled; Bill, poor shaggy titan, would never know the satisfactions of true love. 'You don't understand, Bill,' I said. 'All that's over.'

Bill laughed outright. 'Man's capacity for self-deception astounds me,' he said.

From one professed existentialist to another, an accusation of self-deception was a serious one. The term was a rendering of Sartre's *mauvaise foi*—literally translated as 'bad faith'—and it spotlighted the cardinal sin in the existentialist ethic, man's tendency to lie to himself for the sake of comfort or convenience or to suppress recognition of the full implications of a situation in order to enjoy an immediate advantage. Bill's accusation was comparable with charging a cardinal with heresy.

I took it with suitable gravity. 'There's no self-deception about it,' I said. 'As you know, one of my fundamental beliefs is that "the unexamined life is not worth living", and I tell you I've examined this idea and my motives very carefully before coming to a decision.'

'But you're in no fit state to judge your motives or the situation,' Bill objected. 'On your own admission, you're in love. That means that your senses and judgment are temporarily deranged.'

'Bill's right,' Tom said. 'The examined life is fine as an ideal— a bit dull, perhaps, but worthy—but the question is, who examines the examiner?'

'No,' Bill said, 'the question is, should Stuart bring Carol to live here?'

'I didn't bring it up as a matter of discussion,' I said. 'I'm just telling you what I've decided.'

Bill shrugged. 'So we can't dissuade you. I should have thought your own experience might, though. After all, you've been married once.'

'This isn't the same,' I said.

'Perhaps,' Bill said, 'but it'll be almost as difficult to get out of, supposing you ever want to, and if you don't it *will* be a marriage, won't it?' He smiled, pleased with the irrefutability of his logic.

'Marriage,' Tom said, 'was best defined by Ambrose Bierce as "a community consisting of a master, a mistress and two slaves, making in all, two." '

Bill laughed. '*Touché*, Tom, *touché*,' he said.

Well, the Devil always has the best lines, but though the sequel was as disastrous as Bill and Tom predicted I don't see it as a vindication either of cynicism or of the view that the artist is necessarily a 'prodigious womaniser' off duty and an aloof spiritual colossus on. Both views are too cosy and final. Look closer at any view that facilitates the striking of an attitude, the taking of a stance. Man's hunger is not for truth but for the fixation of belief. Give him a coat that proclaims him 'Cynic' or 'Artist' and he will wear its colours confidently and with pride. Which is not to malign Tom and Bill. My coat boasted the motto 'Lover'. The question was whether I should take Carol to live at the house, but what we were really talking about was love, and none of us knew very much about it. 'Cynic', 'Artist' and 'Lover' were triple moun-tain peaks, wreathed with cloud and capped with ice, within view of each other on a good day, but permanently immovable. Only I fancied that I stood so much higher, knew so much better, for I was more passionate, more daring, more life-affirming. I had no conception of the pain that lay behind Tom's cynicism. He had once been married and had had a house and a well-paid job in the Central Office of Information, and had had his world shattered by the breakdown of his marriage. During the Chepstow Road days he was just putting the pieces of his life together again. I didn't know about any of this until much later. I regarded Tom as an amusing, generous but rather superficial cynic. I knew nothing about pain, nothing about love.

Yet at the time I was proposing to write a book called *The Dialectics of Despair*. I had it all worked out in chapter headings and notes, the 'human condition' tabulated and analysed, and the way beyond despair, the way to a 'higher integration' clearly mapped. In the book would be paraded for the edification of the parochial English all the great themes of existentialism: the death of God, the problem of subjectivism, the elusiveness of reality, the otherness of nature, the illusoriness of freedom, the sense of the absurdity of existence, dualism, angst, and in the last chapter a way out would be shown, a way that Kierkegaard, Nietzsche, Sartre and the rest had not had the will or the insight to find for themselves. I wasn't entirely clear what the way out was, but I was confident that it would emerge in the writing and would have something to do with the reinstatement of God, of love as a vital, unifying force, and of a philosophy that rejected Cartesian doubt and solipsism as its starting point and regarded man and nature as many-faceted wholes involved in an evolutionary process of growth. It was to be a great, sweeping definitive book, but it never got written, for suddenly life, love and pain became more real.

I had a lighter, but connected, literary project on at about this time, part of which actually got written but never appeared in print. It was a long story entitled 'The Man Who Couldn't Despair'. I put the hero through the whole gamut of literary suffering: betrayal, torrid love affairs, brooding guilt, solitariness, alienation, persecution, but endowed him with a faculty that enabled him to rise above it all, to experience moments of vision, of joy, of life affirmation that quite cancelled out the rest. I conceived it as a philosophical comedy. It was the poorest, the saddest, the most desperate thing that I ever wrote. At that time, conscious of no weakness, no fears, no vulnerability, no desperation in myself, I fancied that I wrote out of my strength. I had no conception of the traumas, the shuddering shocks that can negate life utterly. Looking back, I see myself then, as others saw me at the time, with mixed feelings of wonder, pity and awe. I went through hell, but didn't particularly notice it.

My marriage lasted four years, but it began to crack after two. The successful bit was when Anne and I were linked with Alfred Reynolds. There was parallel growth then for a while. We went to Germany for a month in the summer of '53, to the home of a Baron Wolf von Gudenberg, who was one of Alfred's wartime converts to 'the Bridge'. About twenty English and German 'Bridge' enthusiasts stayed in the baron's ancestral home near Kassel, a large ramshackle wood and plaster building with bare wooden floors and heavy furniture which afforded a marvellously congenial atmosphere for a gathering of impecunious philosophers with anarchistic leanings. The sun shone every day and we ate substantial peasant meals, swam in a nearby lake, met for discussions and sing-songs on the verandah in the daytime or before a log fire at night; Anne was the prettiest girl there and I was proud of her and made love to her every night and sometimes in the afternoons too, and it was altogether idyllic. When we left we hitch-hiked down to Koblenz, then up the Rhine, staying in youth hostels, and although Kassel, Frankfurt, Cologne and Düsseldorf were wastelands of rubble the German people were friendly and the sun shone and many of the country roads were lined with fruit trees and there was abundance in the shops too; the 'Bridge' philosophy of sanity and brotherly love and of evil as the product only of wicked ideologies seemed relevant and true and a brave new world of peace and amity seemed not too remote.

Anne blamed Colin Wilson for the break-up of our marriage. He wasn't in fact to blame, but his influence was catalytic. Before I met Colin, I had begun to get dissatisfied both with the 'Bridge' philosophy and with my marriage, because neither seemed to be getting anywhere. I felt trapped in time. I even had hire-purchase commitments for furniture. Colin, when we met, had just got out of his marriage. He had left his wife and son in Leicester and cycled down to London with a rucksack full of books and manuscripts. He had got life down to simple essentials. He slept out in the open in a sleeping-bag, worked in the British Museum reading-room during the day, and travelled all over London by bicycle, visiting friends, attending meetings, giving talks. Also he had three or four girl friends, one of whom, Caroline, was a strikingly pretty blonde. To me, with my furniture, my flat, my two-year-old marriage, my discussions on Tuesdays and sex on Saturdays and just occasionally some other day, Colin's seemed a most enviable life. In the light of it I examined my own, and I felt increasingly as the months went by that I had settled for too little, made too few demands upon myself. Colin introduced me to Bill, who was loquacious, positive and dynamic. There was heady talk, about genius and mediocrity, the cultivation of the will, the demands and responsibilities of leadership, and I began to abhor my furniture that I hadn't yet paid for, my regency-striped wallpaper that made my sitting-room resemble a barred cage, and my cosy, contained life. I began to long for a life of austerity punctuated with interludes of riotous sensuality.

I celebrated my twenty-first birthday with a party at the flat. Colin brought Caroline along. Alfred and several of the 'Bridge' people were there, and Bill; there were some twenty-five to thirty people in all in the small flat, so that the party spread through all the rooms, including the kitchen and bedroom. We drank beer, cider and cheap wine and listened to music and talked, and late in the evening I found myself sitting on the bed talking earnestly to Caroline about her ambition to be a singer, and then Colin looked in and laughed, switched the light off and pulled the door to, and within minutes I was oblivious of the party, with a compliant woman in my arms who responded passionately. Then Anne suddenly came in and switched on the light and instantly started shouting abuse and trying to get at Caroline, but I stood in the way, until Alfred intervened and took Anne away to the kitchen, where they remained for half an hour while the other embarrassed guests dispersed. Before they left, Colin said, 'Never mind, she'll get over it,' and Caroline apologised and said she didn't know what had got into her, and Colin laughed and said he thought *I* had. Then they were all gone and I was alone in my sitting-room, with the striped wallpaper and new three-piece suite, feeling wretched at the outcome of the evening but at the same time elated at the memory of my first erotic adventure since I came to London. There would be other occasions, there would be consummations; of that I was sure, and in my certainty I could be conciliatory, even contrite, to Anne, who had now stopped sobbing and was being soothed in the kitchen by Alfred's soft middle-European voice, which was such a perfect instrument for taking the edges off the harsh realities of life and putting problems into a philosophical perspective.

'I am very fond of both of you,' Alfred said when he brought a chastened Anne out of the kitchen, 'and it would break my heart to see you separate. So be reconciled, my friends. Anne is deeply hurt, Stuart. She needs your help and your love, and you will give it to her, I know. I have explained to her. I think she understands that it signified nothing. But she is hurt and it will take time for the hurt to heal.'

He took our hands and joined them and I looked into Anne's hurt eyes and felt tears prickle in my own, but they were not tears of contrition; they welled up at the thought that I was going to hurt this girl, my boyhood sweetheart who had followed me down to London when I sent for her, a hell of a lot more before we finally parted, as we inevitably must.

So I broke free, had a series of mistresses, including Caroline, and when Anne got involved with the poet Michael Hastings I took myself off to Germany for three months to let them get on with it. It was a fairly painless disintegration of a marriage. What seems strangest about that time in retrospect is that apart from that first occasion, no one showed the least sign of sexual jealousy. We got to the point, before I went to Germany, where Anne would quite happily go out to see a film or visit a friend if I told her I needed the bedroom for the evening. We considered we were being civilised and rational. We regarded sex as one of the pleasures of life, to be enjoyed like a good meal, and had come to accept that variety was its spice. We had Eros tamed and domesticated, no longer mighty and godlike with the power to drive a man to madness or death for jealousy or love, but now on a par with the *lares* and *penates*, the little household gods.

'We're more like brother and sister,' I would explain when some girlfriend expressed surprise that I should be on such good terms with my wife and her lover. And it was true. Having grown up together and come down to London and gone through years of hardship, we had a relationship that we felt couldn't be abruptly terminated. When I returned from Germany and went to live at the house in Chepstow Road, leaving Michael and Anne in the Hampstead flat, I continued to see them frequently. I was a sort of brother, or even father-figure, to both of them for a time, and would reconcile them when they quarrelled, as they often did, and be a confidant to each of them separately. And I confided in Anne, at least I did until the affair with Carol started. I had to assure her then that I had no intention of marrying Carol.

Carol understood that too. Our love was spiritual, it didn't need ratifying by Church or State.

We had very serious conversations. I gave her Tolstoy and Dostoevski and Hesse to read and we talked about their books and about religion and God.

We were both a bit God-obsessed. Carol had read St Teresa of Avila and she said she could understand the appeal of a life of devotion to God.

'Even if it meant taking a vow of chastity?'

We had this conversation over a table in Jimmy the Greek's dim basement restaurant in Soho after eating a plate of Jimmy's excellent stuffed vine leaves.

'I must admit I'd find that very difficult,' Carol admitted. She smiled and reached across the table and took my hand.

'It's not necessary,' I said. 'Sex too can be a form of worship.'

'Oh yes, I feel that,' Carol said. 'Though when the church people say "God is love" that isn't what they have in mind, is it?'

'No, they mean benevolence or forgiveness. But the religion of the Churches has always been concerned primarily with reconciling Man to his unhappy lot. Do you know St Augustine's sentence: "Thou hast made us for Thyself, and our heart is restless until it rests in Thee." '

'That's beautiful.'

'Yes, but what is this "rest" that God confers on those who love Him? It's not a state of respite, retirement, inactivity, or release from "the weariness, the fever and the fret" of life. When I'm at one with God I'm not at rest, I'm participating in His creative activity, I have tremendous energies. I'm not escaping from reality but entering more deeply into it.'

'Yes,' Carol said. She was an avid listener when I talked like this. Before I met her she had been thinking of getting baptised. I had dissuaded her.

Now she was frowning slightly. 'But does this mean that God is just a force of nature?' she said. 'I mean, you can't love an impersonal force, can you?'

The restaurant was full and a waiter gave me the bill, obviously hoping that we'd go. I ordered two more cups of tea. 'No, I'm not preaching a naive vitalism,' I said, leaning closer to Carol across the table so as not to be overheard. 'I believe that God is both immanent and transcendent, both existence and essence. He can be loved in His immanence, through man and nature, which is the way most of us love Him, or in His transcendence, which is the way of the mystic. You know the lines of Blake's Angel:

"Little creature born of joy and mirth,
Go love without the help of any Thing on earth."

Well, that's the mystic's way and it's difficult. That's your St Teresa.'

'And the other way?'

'The other way is to love the Creator through His creation, and to participate in the process of creation. For me all love is physical.'

If Bill had witnessed that scene, he would have hooted with laughter. He was convinced that I used the spiritual approach to get girls to bed. 'It's your soul I'm really interested in, says Stuart, as he expertly unfastens the girl's bra,' Bill would say when there was a crowd of people around and he wanted to get at me. This sort of raillery was a kind of sport among us.

He and Tom soon got used to having Carol about the house. She was unobtrusive and she made tea and boiled eggs and she was gay and interested in all the talk and the schemes. Usually the day began with tea and the day's papers in Tom's room between eleven o'clock and midday. Tom would be in carpet slippers, with a short red silk dressing-gown over his pyjamas, and Bill would appear, unshaven and uncombed, in shirt and trousers that he might have slept in, and they would smoke cigarettes and discuss the papers, appraising them with the eyes of professionals, comparing the different treatments of subjects, the choice of lead stories, the make-up of front pages, tracing where a story 'broke' and how it was taken up by other papers, and pointing out who had managed to get into and who had been left out of the gossip columns. It was all a bit technical for me to contribute much, but Carol and I usually joined them, read the news and listened to their commentaries. I wasn't a smoker at the time, and I usually ate two boiled eggs because I'd read somewhere that after sex one needed protein to refortify the gonads. Carol learnt to boil eggs just as I liked them, soft but not slimy.

A great disappointment to all of us was that Bill's theatrical project didn't get off the ground. He had had the financial backing all lined up, he said, but he hadn't been able to reach an agreement with the owners of the theatre about the terms of the lease. The falling-through of the scheme put him in Fleet Street's bad books for a time, for the press had given it a good deal of publicity, and he found it difficult to get anything in the papers, though Tom did all he could in his column. It was Bill's firm belief that 'we must keep our names before the public', and he gnashed his teeth and got quite eloquently malicious when such as Lady Lewisham, Billy Graham, Liberace, the 'Chelsea set' or Russian space dogs seemed to be getting all the publicity. However, he had a project brewing that they would all have to sit up and take notice of, he said, though as yet it was too early to tell even his closest friends about it. Meanwhile, we would throw in our lot with the English Stage Company at the Royal Court so far as theatrical work was concerned, and as a platform for our ideas we would use the columns of *Time and Tide*, the editor of which was hospitable to 'angry young men' who would write for three or four guineas a thousand.

Bill would enthusiastically assent to the proposition that 'what we need today is a new religion,' but he wasn't, as Carol and I were, God-obsessed. I suppose the idea of participating in the creation of a new religion appealed to him because the work called for superman efforts, heroics, martyrdoms, militancy, publicity, but neither God nor love had any place in his idea of a religion. Once during the first weeks when Carol was living with me I took her and Bill to a weekend conference on 'The Search for Meaning', at which I'd been invited to speak. It was held at an R.A.F. college because some high-ranking R.A.F. officer had taken up religion in his retirement and was a prominent member of the Centre for Religious and Spiritual Studies, which put on the programme.

'You must be joking,' Bill said when I asked him to go with us. 'Do you mean to say that people will actually spend a weekend in the sticks in midwinter hoping to discover the meaning of life?'

'All expenses paid for me and any guests I want to take,' I said.

'Well, I suppose it'll be an experience,' Bill said.

'Of monumental irrelevance,' Tom said; 'but you should go, Bill, because you're always knocking people for not asking fundamental questions. Here's a batch that do, and I hope they bore you rigid.'

They did. Bill, Carol and I sat through a series of lectures and discussions on the first day in which psychiatrists, theologians and scientists concurred that love was the answer to the problem of the meaning of life.

'A bunch of bloody mediocrities,' Bill said as we ate in a brightly-lit refectory that evening.

'I agree with you, Bill,' I said. 'But the funny thing is that they're right. The only trouble is that with them it's the *idea* of love that is an answer to the *idea* of meaninglessness.'

'They don't know either state as an existential reality,' said Carol, who had picked up the jargon by now.

'You're all fools,' Bill said, 'and this is the most meaningless weekend that I've ever spent. The only existential realities are will, power, energy.'

'I hail the superhuman,' I declaimed.

'I wish you did,' Bill said. 'It seems to me you're turning Christian, or worse, reverting to the tepid humanism of old Alfred What's-his-name in Dollis Hill, with his, "We must love one another or die." '

'It was Auden who wrote that.'

'He's another one. Look what happened to the 'thirties. A generation of maudlin mediocrities. All they proved is that you can love one another *and* die.'

I had to give my speech on the morning of the second day. I spoke from notes that I had jotted down the night before. The Air-Marshal introduced me as an 'angry young man' and the audience of about a hundred and fifty settled down, perhaps imagining that they were about to be harangued by a latter-day Savonarola.

'Any comprehensive philosophy must be, among other things, the critic of satisfactions,' I began. 'Unless it can criticise the satisfactoriness of other ideas, a philosophy of meaning is bound to get bogged down in relativism and admit the equal validity of as many meanings as there are people who entertain them. So let me say this at the start: the mental satisfaction is not enough. Man's hunger for meaning cannot be satisfied by knowledge or by scriptural truth. It is hunger for *more life*. Love, we have heard it said, is the answer, the meaning. Yes, but wait. The answer to what? Merely to a question: what is the meaning of life? No, that's not good enough. No concept of meaning has any validity that is not hard won from a vision of meaninglessness.'

I went on to expound my own 'vision of meaninglessness'. 'He gave them a dose of the old existentialist horrorshow,' Bill reported to Tom when we got back to Chepstow Road in the evening, 'and they loved every minute of it.'

'Of course they did,' Tom said. 'The God-hungry are always gluttons for punishment. They're masochists before they find Him, which is bad enough, but they turn into sadists afterwards. Just look at that.' He pointed at the picture of 'The Penitent', the kneeling naked girl surrounded by grim nuns. 'God preserve me from the godly!'

'That's a prayer, Tom, be careful,' I laughed.

'A rhetorical one, Stuart, I assure you. I know very well that *I* have to do the preserving. All I ask is that nobody interferes with my happy sins in the holy name of what might not exist.'

'I agree with you about the godly, Tom,' Bill said, 'but what *do* you believe in?'

Tom plucked his long cigarette-holder from his mouth and frowned. 'It's not a line we sell. You must remember that I'm Lucifer's faithful servant. We don't recommend the wares of the Other Place. In fact we do our humble best to dissuade people from trading in life, fun and beauty for a spurious promissory note which anyway only promises an eternity of tedium among the righteous and the godly.'

'But Tom,' Bill said, 'people with your views find *this* life tedious. A man has to have an obsession, and none of the things you profess to believe in are worthy of being obsessive about.'

'You damn well leave my beliefs alone,' Tom said. 'I don't mind

53

a man having obsessions, so long as he doesn't thrust them down my throat. "Worthy" indeed! You know, with your value judgments you belong among the godly party. And, for your information, I don't find this life tedious. I enjoy every minute of it.'

'But enjoyment isn't good enough, Tom,' Bill said. 'The question is, what do you hope to achieve?'

'Hope to? I've achieved it.'

'What?'

'The complete life.'

Bill laughed. 'Then isn't it about time you died?'

'Not at all. I said "complete", not "completed".'

'Sophistry, Tom. In a man without purpose the will dies, and a man without will is a vegetable.'

In discussions of this kind, Bill would sit back in his chair and smile when he had made a point. Tom, by contrast, was all movement and gesture, and would frequently get up and walk about the room. He jumped up from his chair now and crossed to the desk where he searched among a litter of papers.

'Just let me read you a couple of stanzas from a recent little composition of mine,' he said.

Bill sank in his chair. 'The man doesn't write for publication, but for persecution,' he said.

Tom paced the room and recited his lines with vigour, making little stabbing gestures in the air with his cigarette-holder:

'Is Man no more than what he is—a Man
Slow dragging out his unimportant span?
No punishment, no hope, and no reward;
No good, no bad, no Devil and no Lord?

Then let us part-existence justify
With just one bright and self-convincing Lie,
For smallness does not fit this mortal scheme,
Where Truth itself is swallowed by the Dream.'

'What you're in fact advocating is bad faith,' Bill said.

'I call it the Necessary Illusion,' Tom said. 'To me, faiths are neither good nor bad, neither true nor untrue. They're just necessary.'

'For others, but not for you,' I said.

54

'I tell you, I believe in beauty and brandy. One needs fewer illusions as one gets older. And you must always remember that I'm a thousand years old.'

'And you don't look a day over fifty,' Bill said.

Such was the mood and tone of those late-night discussions in Tom's room. We laughed a lot, mocked each other, scored points, but the issues were fundamentally serious ones. Carol listened attentively, and though she rarely contributed she often took up points with me afterwards when we were alone. 'I've learnt so much in these weeks,' she said once.

Carol had had a 'steady' boy friend down in Kent for a couple of years before we met, and for weeks after moving in with me she worried about whether and what she should tell him. I thought she agitated herself unduly about it and told her simply to write and tell him she'd fallen in love with someone else. It didn't occur to me that there could be any question for her of choosing between us. She did write and tell him in the end, but only, she said, after she'd decided that she wouldn't be able to go back to him even if we split up. 'I'm sorry I've been such a bore about it,' she said after she'd sent the letter,'but he did ask me to marry him.'

'You don't want marriage,' I said. 'You're going to be a great actress.'

Carol was convinced of that too. If only she could get a break, a chance to show her worth. She was out two or three times a week seeing her agent or attending auditions, but the hoped-for break remained elusive. 'Oh, I wish I could show you how good I can be,' she said. 'I'd like to do Saint Joan.'

'You will one day,' I assured her, but when she kept getting turned down I began to wonder.

I began to get a bit impatient too. I had envisaged our life to-gether as that of two hard-working artists pursuing independent careers. Carol would be out at the theatre in the evenings and perhaps rehearsals in the mornings, and I would have the place to myself and be able to work in peace. We would be together for meals, for a bit of socialising, and to make love, and life for each of us would be full and eventful and we'd have a lot to talk about, spending so much of our time in different worlds. That was how I'd imagined it would be.

55

'You're so lucky,' she said, 'being able to use your talents without being dependent on anyone else. All you need is a quiet room and a typewriter.' I was sympathetic and reassuring.

'You must find it a bore, having us around all the time,' she said another time. The "us" meant her and Mr Gilbert, the Peke. If any proof were needed of the depth of my love for Carol it lay, to my mind, in the fact that I'd taken in her dog as well. And it was the dog that I first fell out of love with. At first he'd wanted to sleep on the foot of our bed and I'd kept kicking him off until he got the message that if he wanted a good night's sleep he'd have to have it somewhere else. Carol hadn't protested about that. But Mr Gilbert had other bad habits. He rushed about aimlessly and excitedly and got under my feet, he yapped whenever he heard anyone on the stairs, and about twice a week he wandered off down Chepstow Road and we had to get together a search party to find him. After about a month of this I broke off diplomatic relations with Mr Gilbert. I refused to buy his Kennomeat and to join the search parties. After about six weeks I opened hostilities, aiming surreptitious kicks at him and throwing his little hard rubber ball directly at his nose instead of across the room.

But it wasn't only the dog. After a couple of months I began to get irritated with Carol. She talked too much about the theatre and boring theatrical people and when she sat reading for long hours she was 'being a good girl and letting me work'. The work wasn't going too well, either. How do you write about 'The Despair of Europe' (Chapter One of *The Dialectics of Despair*) when you're continually being driven to desperation by a bloody pekinese? One needed detachment, objectivity, conditions conducive to the contemplative life, to do justice to such a theme. I didn't for a moment imagine that I was falling out of love with Carol. I thought it was just that we were living too cramped a life, seeing too much of each other. When an opportunity arose to get away for a couple of weeks I jumped at it.

Among the occasional visitors to the house was a writer named Paul Rowland. He had a cottage in Sussex which he could only use in school holidays, for he was a resident teacher in a private school. He happened to come round one evening and to mention that the cottage was available for any of us who felt like getting away from London for a while to enjoy 'the eternal sanities of nature' (he talked like that), and he was delighted when I said I'd like to take up the offer.

Carol understood. She said something about knowing that if she wanted to hold me she would have to do so loosely and on a long rein, and so, tenuously tethered and loosely held, I went to the country to work.

The journey from Charing Cross was like a liberation. It was a cold, clear, still day at the beginning of December. There had been a light fall of snow during the night and south of Tunbridge Wells the fields were still white in patches. The forests of the Weald were a symphony of shades of green and brown, with here and there a patch of flaming red, and when I contemplated the vistas of rolling country from the train window I felt a sustained joy. One forgot how stifling London was, how rarely one experienced there a spasm of sheer simple delight in things seen.

Paul Rowland's cottage was a half-hour's bus journey from a small country station. When I got off the bus, following Paul's directions, I could see the cottage down in a valley, two fields away from the road. There were woods on two sides of it, and on the green hill rising beyond it a copse of dark trees stood out sharply against the skyline. Paul had told me where the key was hidden, and had given me detailed written instructions about the domestic arrangements. Water had to be fetched in buckets from a stream some fifty yards away. It was quite pure, because it came from a spring just a little further upstream. Light was provided by paraffin lamps, which had to be handled carefully so that the mantles shouldn't break. There was a wide, open fireplace with a stack of dry logs beside it, and there was plenty more fuel to be found in the surrounding woods. The village stores was about a mile away by the short cut over the fields. In a cupboard in the kitchen I would find sugar, tea, coffee and some cans of evaporated milk, stewed steak, beans and sausages.

It was already getting dark when I arrived. The cottage had been empty for weeks but it still smelled of woodsmoke and paraffin. I soon got a fire going and the oil lamps lit, and made myself a meal of sausages and beans. I spent the evening reading in front of the log fire and before turning in took a walk along the paths through the woods. The ground was crunchy with frost underfoot and the sky above was clear and brilliant with stars, which seemed so much closer than they ever did in London. When I went to bed I left a window open, and I was lulled to sleep by the sound of the steady rush of water.

The conditions were ideal for the contemplative, creative life. I got up the following morning feeling full of joy and vitality and ideas, and eager to get to grips with the problems of 'The Despair of Europe'. I had intended to begin with, and had already written, a chapter analysing despair in the Romantics, but now my ideas began to range wider. Why not, I thought, do a depth analysis of the European consciousness, tracing it back to its origins in the pre-Christian Hebraic and Hellenic cultures? Solomon and Job would serve as symbolic figures to start with, representing two distinct varieties of despair, temperamental and circumstantial. Solomon, with his 'he who increases knowledge increases sorrow', suggested a formula that would apply throughout the book: the more consciousness, the more despair. And Job, with his cry, 'Where is judgment to be found, and where is the place of understanding?' expressed a form of despair very familiar to modern man: that which followed from the perception that there is no stable moral order. What Solomon and Job had in common was a feeling of alienation. Solomon, the highly developed, highly conscious man, felt alienated from reality and from his true self. For him, both the life of the mind and the life of the senses had proved equally dissatisfying. He had everything, and yet longed for something more, he knew not what, which would give him a sense of reality and identity. Job's case was different. His despair was not a subjective condition, it stemmed from the fact that for him the universe was suddenly divested of sense and meaning. He felt alienated from God and from the moral law.

It was good to have the ideas flowing again. I worked hard for several days, developing my theme, writing about fifteen hundred words a day. I took breaks from writing to collect and chop wood, carry water from the stream, walk to the village stores, prepare and eat meals. I enjoyed the chores, particularly the woodchopping, which I did with a long-handled axe. To aim and swing it accurately required skill, a good eye and a steady hand, and to split a log clean down the middle with one blow was very satisfying. I felt in peak physical and mental condition.

My condition suggested another formula which led to further

ramifications of my analysis: despair is a failure of self-affirmation. A man needs, I argued, to affirm himself existentially, spiritually and morally, and when he is prevented from any or all of these forms of self-affirmation he is in despair. His existential self-affirmation is threatened by death, his spiritual self-affirmation by the threat of meaninglessness, and his moral self-affirmation by the threat of sin and condemnation. And the fact that the problems of death, meaninglessness and condemnation figure so prominently in modern literature is evidence, if any is needed, of the despair of Europe. They are problems, moreover, to which only religion can offer a solution.

On the weekend Paul Rowland turned up unexpectedly. I felt irritated at having to interrupt my work, but I could hardly make Paul unwelcome in his own cottage.

Paul was the elder of two brothers, both in their forties, who had been brought up by a father ambitious to make English gentlemen of them and a mother who had been convinced that they had a unique vocation for sainthood. The stresses that their parents' irreconcilable ambitions had set up in them had remained with them for life. When their father died they squandered their considerable patrimony in a manner befitting gentlemanly English reprobates, then proceeded to pursue austere, saintly lives in remote cottages. Paul, however, had been more consistent and truer to his mother's memory, for the younger brother, Brian, had got married two years before. He was living in his in-laws' house in Battle, a village about six miles away from the cottage, and Paul suggested that we might go over and see him on the Sunday. 'I'd like you to meet, and you might find it useful to have someone you can talk to in the district,' he said.

Brian Rowland, I thought when I met him, looked older than his brother. He was thin and ill-looking and wore baggy brown corduroys and a grey sweater that was too big for his small frame and full of holes.

The brothers clearly enjoyed each other's company. Both of them were clever raconteurs and they spent most of the day telling funny stories to each other and to an admiring crowd that gathered round them in the local pub at lunch time. I watched, listened and laughed, but throughout the day my attention was really focused on Sue, Brian's wife.

59

I was accustomed to seeing silent, domesticated, background wives and was in the habit of completely ignoring them. Sue kept in the background, said little, attended to her eighteen-month-old baby, made meals, tea, coffee, and seemed every bit a little wife doing her duties. But there was something about her that proclaimed a difference, an independence. It was in the way she listened and looked on as the men talked, with an air of detached amusement. It was in the way she went about her work, the way she sat and smoked her little cigars. My antennae picked up the message that this marriage was on the rocks.

Throughout the day, while the brothers talked and joked, Sue and I stole looks at each other that held for me a vertiginous promise.

'Come and help me pick some spinach for supper,' she said to me in the evening.

It was getting dark. The 'garden' was more like a wilderness of long grass, brambles, and looming fruit-trees. Sue had a torch. 'I'll lead the way,' she said, and took my hand.

Her hand was hot, dry and rather rough. It was a long slender hand without much flesh on the bones. I found the feel of it strangely exciting.

We ducked under some low branches and emerged into an open area where the ridged earth indicated that there had once been a vegetable garden.

'The spinach is around here somewhere,' Sue said.

We both looked around at the indistinguishable undergrowth and laughed. I took her other hand, drew her closer and gazed into her eyes.

'You're very lovely,' I said. 'I've been looking at you all day.'

'Yes, I noticed. Your eyes have been positively burning me up.'

Her eyes had a disturbed look. She tried to draw her hands away, but I held them tighter and she didn't resist. Nor did she resist when I kissed her, though she reciprocated the kiss with only the merest tremor of consent. I tried to take a firmer grip on her, draw her body against mine and make her mouth open wider. She broke away and said breathlessly, 'We must get the spinach. They'll wonder what's happened to us.'

We found the spinach. A lot of it had run to seed. As we picked the leaves she went on talking as if nothing had happened. Her father had bought the bungalow when they returned from India in '47. It wasn't a very pretty house, but he had bought it for the four acres of land. He had wanted to keep chickens—'You can't keep a retired army officer and a chicken apart'—but then he had taken a job with the army in Germany, and since he had left nobody had attended to the land, which had steadily reverted to jungle. The police had once found that a far corner of it was being used as a dump for stolen petrol!

I listened sulkily and picked spinach and wondered what the hell the bitch thought she was doing with me. She had led me on all day with her looks, had contrived this expedition into the jungle, and now she was keeping me at bay with her bright chatter. When she decided that we had picked enough spinach, I tried again.

'We're not going back until you let me kiss you again,' I said.

'Alright,' she said, 'but only if you promise to hold all the spinach and not to drop it.'

I said, 'I promise.'

But this time she kissed me. While I clutched an armful of spinach she insinuated slender arms around my neck, exerted pressure on the back of my head and neck with nervous, bony fingers, and planted on my lips an inexpressibly tender yet firm kiss which shuddered through me like an electric shock. But she made it brief and then stepped back a pace.

'There you are,' she said, 'you unscrupulous seducer of other men's wives.' But she was smiling and there was no reproach in the words.

That night back at the cottage, I couldn't sleep for thinking of her. I went over the daytime and again in my mind, remembering the looks she had given me, her tender kiss, the feel of her curiously rough hands. And I remembered telling Carol some time before that I didn't want anyone else because with her for the first time in my experience sex and love had come together. And it had been true at the time.

The ephemerality of love. Poets have celebrated it, our contemporary youth culture celebrates it. To seek an enduring love is to want an ignoble settlement with life, to purchase ease at the cost of intensity, adventure, freedom. The lover as hero is the man who moves from conquest to conquest, who never puts down roots, who has the resilience to celebrate the agonies of love as well as its joys. He values freedom above all, and one is never so free as with the new potential lover, a stranger, for one can choose oneself anew, a mask to wear, a personality to project.

It had been like that with Carol. I was the great writer, she the great actress. Ours had to be a great love affair. It was a strain to keep it up. There was domesticity, the dog, the problem of money, Carol's failure to get work, the unglamorous day-to-day struggle with words and ideas. To Sue I was the unscrupulous seducer, the literary Casanova from the big bad city who came into her life one Sunday and bulldozed through the proprieties and her inhibitions. It wasn't exactly a new identity. I had lived the life of the sexual freebooter between splitting with Anne and getting involved with Carol. But it was a relief to get back to the role and to confess to myself that the demanding eternal love bit was after all an illusion.

I didn't see any more of Sue at this time. I'd only been at the cottage a few days when a letter came from Carol saying she'd got a small part and a job as stage manager in a touring company, starting at Leeds the following Monday. So I went up to London on the Saturday and we had one night together. I didn't say anything, she was so excited about the job.

It is a craven, ill-judged and cruel stratagem to try to substitute kindness for love. But that's what I did. Carol was only able to pay occasional visits to London in the ensuing weeks, when her show came within striking distance, so I reckoned that I could keep up the pretence that things between us were as they had been for as long as she kept the job. I thought that with separation and the passing of time her own ardour might abate and the final break become easier. And I felt that after losing her mother and becoming alienated from her father, it would be too great a blow for her to be abruptly dropped by her first lover. Also there was a chance that she might meet somebody else while on tour. Thus I debated the situation with myself, worrying over fine points of morality while continuing to commit the major sin of still sleeping with a woman I no longer loved and hoping for some turn of events that would accomplish my deliverance without leaving me with the pain of a guilty conscience.

I formed a number of undemanding liaisons while Carol was on tour, but always kept myself free for her visits. Until on one occasion she arrived without previous warning.

It was a Saturday night and Bill and I were at a party. I had picked up a psychology student from Birkbeck College. We danced together for a bit, then removed ourselves to a dim corner, and before long we had reached a point where the party seemed rather overcrowded, so I suggested that we might return to my place. Bill saw us leaving and joined us. He was never a man of tact; he regarded it as a virtue of the pusillanimous. Also it was a kind of game with him to spike my guns.

When we got back to the house he suggested a cup of tea in Tom's room. It was as well that he did. Tom managed to get across to me the message that Carol had arrived and had gone to bed because she was tired after the journey. Bill watched my discomfiture with amusement. His look said, 'Let's see you wriggle out of this!' It was too late for the girl to get a bus or tube back to Highgate, where she lived, and I hadn't enough money for a taxi. Fortunately, the conversation with Bill and Tom reduced the temperature a bit, and I seized the opportunity to make out that it was the pleasure of intellectual rather than carnal intercourse that I sought from her. I developed a sudden interest in her psychological studies. It was lucky that the spare room was empty that weekend. When at last the conversation flagged and Tom said he wanted to get some sleep I took the girl down there and settled her down for the night with an elaborate show of chivalrous solicitude for her comfort, which clearly bewildered her. As I trudged back up the stairs to my room, Bill leaned over the banisters above and said, 'Crafty bastard! But you won't get away with it. You'll be dragged down to hell, there to burn for a million years alongside Don Giovanni.'

I said, 'And a damn fine faithful Leporello you make, Hopkins.' Bill went away chuckling.

I felt fagged out, and I experienced what is commonly described as a sinking feeling but what felt more like my entire inner works collapsing into the pit of my stomach and messily coalescing there when I saw Carol brightly sitting up in bed reading.

'You're late, darling,' she said. She put down her book on the bedside table and held out her arms, and I called on resources I didn't know I possessed for my second act of spurious chivalry within the space of five minutes.

We worked it out later that that must have been the time when she got pregnant.

Carol's show folded after a few weeks and she returned to London. I couldn't go to Sussex because Paul was using his cottage over the Christmas holiday, so I phoned Colin to see if I could have the use of the chalet in his garden for a few weeks. I told Carol that I really had to work full stretch on the book now. She was visibly less enthusiastic than when I'd left for Sussex, but she didn't demur.

I remember walking along a cliff path, with Colin ahead of me pushing a bicycle. I had met him in the Fountain. His car was being repaired and he had cycled over to Mevagissey to meet me. I'd arrived by train at St Austell and taken the bus into Mevagissey. When we left the Fountain it was getting dark and when we'd gone about half a mile a light drizzle began to fall. In the pub all our talk had been of writing and books, but as we were walking along the cliff path Colin shouted out, 'I'm glad you didn't bring Carol with you this time. Is that all over?'

'Pretty well,' I shouted back into the wind, 'though she's living in my room at the moment.'

'So Bill told me. I thought that was a fatal move. Still, you can stay down here as long as you like. I'm off to the States next month, so you'll be able to have the whole place to yourself. What are you working on now?'

'The Despair book's coming on, and I've got about half a play written.'

'That's good. We've got to keep churning the stuff out. Make them take notice.'

We walked on in silence for a bit until the path widened and we could walk abreast.

'I'm sorry if I was a bit curmudgeonly about Carol when you were down last,' Colin said. 'What it comes down to, I suppose, is that we've different ideas of the function of women. I'm more of an egotist than you. I need a woman to make me human again, not to remind me that we both have minds. Do you know those lines of Heine's:

64

"Your body's love I still desire,
For it is young and fair,
Your soul can go and hang itself,
I've soul enough to spare." '

'I suppose I hoped that with Carol something more than just a physical relationship would have been possible,' I said.

'You're a romantic,' Colin said.

'I suppose so,' I agreed. 'I still believe that a really profound relationship with a woman can add a dimension to a man's life that he couldn't otherwise achieve.'

'I dunno, Stuart,' Colin said; 'any man who needs anything added to his life is pretty well a dead loss.' Colin had a special tone of voice for such statements, casual but at the same time lamenting. He always prefaced his more outrageous assertions with 'I dunno'. He went on: 'A man should be able to spend a lifetime just thinking. Women get in the way of a man's thinking, particularly so-called intelligent women with their bright chatter. I should have thought that after splitting with Anne you'd have steered clear of the type for evermore.'

'Carol's not the same type,' I said.

'No, but she gets in your hair just as much, doesn't she?' I couldn't deny it. Colin laughed. 'You know, you should see more of Caroline. Now there's a nice, accommodating, undemanding girl who understands the needs of a man of genius. She asks after you. She never understood why you dropped her so abruptly.'

Caroline was the pretty blonde that Colin had brought to my twenty-first birthday party at the Hampstead flat. I'd been having an affair with her when I met Carol.

'Perhaps I'll look her up when I'm back in town,' I said.

'You should,' he said.

The walk got more arduous. It was uphill, and there were fences and gates to climb and muddy patches to negotiate, and the rain came on heavier. We struggled on in silence for a while. With my rucksack slung on my back I felt like a Pilgrim fleeing from the City of Destruction. I thought of London and Carol and the analogy didn't seem inapt.

Colin insisted on carrying my rucksack for a while, and I pushed his bicycle, which was scarcely less laborious. At last we got to the top of the hill and stopped to rest. A few yards in front of us the cliff fell sheer away. We could hear the crash and drag of the breakers on the rocks below, and from the direction of the great rock-island that loomed a mile out to sea there came the dolorous deep regular clang of the warning bell.

'That's Gorran over there,' Colin said, pointing to a cluster of lights about a mile away. 'It's all downhill from here.'

It was downhill but not without hazards. When we got near the village we had to scramble through hedges, leap ditches, and tramp round the muddy peripheries of ploughed fields. We were both sodden and exhausted when at last we reached the house.

'Why didn't you get a taxi from Meva?' Joy said brightly.

'Because it wasn't fucking raining when we set out,' Colin said. 'And I had my bike with me, didn't I?'

'You could have left it at Lionel's.'

'Well, I didn't. And now I'm wet and hungry, so dig out some food while I have a shower and change.'

'I think you'll find everything you need in the chalet,' Joy said. 'I made up the bed and put the electric fire on this morning, so it should be warm. If you need anything else just give a shout. Of course you'll have all your meals up here with us.'

'Thanks for everything,' I said, and gave her a kiss.

Joy was serene, the soul of equanimity. Colin raged at her one minute and petted her the next, and she bore it all with an air of surprise and humour. She may have seemed the little background woman, but she always looked as if she had a secret, a little inaccessible rock-island inside where she sat and looked out on the world.

Colin was a queer mixture of the ascetic and the *bon viveur*. He spent lavishly on expensive wines, malt whiskies and long-playing records, but cared little what he wore or ate or what his surroundings were like. As his guest, one had to be prepared to drink wine like a Saxon war-lord and at the same time listen to a lecture on philosophy or literature or to a complete performance of some obscure operatic masterpiece that he had recently unearthed. It was a basic tenet of his philosophy that man must strive to be a god and will never attain to the status until he learns to focus his mind like a laser for long periods of time; and it seemed to be a basic function of his hospitality to provide the conditions for practice in such concentration.

66

It was a good atmosphere to work in. We would both write all day, then get together in the evening to read one another's work, listen to music and talk. Colin settled himself in a large armchair by the fire, and as the evening progressed he surrounded himself with piles of books, record sleeves and bottles.

At the end of my first week in Cornwall I had completed the second act of a play. It was based on the diary of a Norwegian Resistance leader who had been captured and imprisoned by the Nazis. A rationalist and an atheist, he came to discover that his values and beliefs were inadequate. He shared a cell with a devout Catholic and a foul-mouthed boorish sailor, both of whom were better able than he to adapt to the humiliation of prison life. The three men represented Body, Soul and Intellect, or so a reviewer informed me some months later when the play was performed. I thought the play was about pain, betrayal, and the break-up and re-integration of a personality. Under torture my hero betrayed other members of the Resistance. His experience brought home to him that intellect and rationalism were inadequate to support the spiritual and moral life of a man when he found himself in an extreme situation. My hero experienced himself as a complete void, a soul with a crying need for God.

'Yes, these are psychological areas that modern English writers don't explore, and they're important, but we've got to get beyond existentialism, Stuart,' Colin said when he read the first two acts of the play. Then he launched into one of his long speeches. He often talked at length and too fast to be interrupted. He wasn't so much giving a lecture, though that is how it must read on the page, but rather pursuing his train of thought. He sat slumped in his armchair, head bowed, chin on chest, brow furrowed, not looking directly at me. The light glinted on the lenses of his glasses.

'The existentialists have got stuck with this image of man inhabiting an alien, meaningless world in which he feels, as Proust said, "accidental, mediocre, mortal". According to Sartre, man *creates* meaning. I'd disagree. I'd say man *perceives* meaning. Meaning is all around us. If we feel "accidental, mediocre, mortal", it's our perception that's at fault. We're functioning at too low a pressure. Sartre is obsessed with the subject of how the gaze of the other person can narrow and distort our sense of identity. It's true that I might experience a distortion of my self-image if I'm caught looking through a keyhole for instance, but to base a whole philosophy on the fact, as Sartre does, is ridiculous. Why not base a philosophy on the opposite experience, on those moments that Maslow calls "peak experiences", when we perceive the wide network of relations between things? Like Yeats sitting at a café table and suddenly feeling that "I was blessed and could bless"? Such experiences show that meaning is not a thing we impose on the world, but is always there, as a reality outside us. Reality is a network of interrelations. Human consciousness is not a blank screen on which we and others project images to distract us from its ultimate blankness. Human consciousness is the perception of these interrelations. A child gets absorbed in a book and his imagination expands until the world becomes a magical place. Sartre would say that he has entered the world of *created* meaning, as artificial as Disneyland. But the relational theory of consciousness would explain his experience as a perception of a wider net of relations, and therefore as a valid experience of reality. In fact, that is the way the world should appear to us all the time, if consciousness operated at its correct pressure. And there's no reason why it shouldn't, except that most men are basically lazy and easily discouraged.'

He went on about 'peak experiences' and Abraham Maslow, an American psychologist whose work he had recently come across and found to have close correspondences with his own. The name was new to me and Colin piled my lap with books and pamphlets to take to the chalet and read over the next few days.

I didn't get through them, though. The following evening Carol rang up and announced that she was pregnant. I reluctantly said I'd go back to London.

3

Carol wanted to go through with it. 'I want *us* to go through with it,' she emphasised. 'You are the father, you know.'

The word made me wince. It made me angry too. It was ridiculous, it was emotional bullying, to drag the idea of fatherhood in. We were talking about a foetus, an unformed, a still disposable thing. My idea of helping Carol was to provide the money for her to have an abortion. It would have to be earned, and probably by uncongenial work. I considered it no small sacrifice, and a fair acquittal of my responsibility in the matter. She said she had known that it was really all over between us when I had gone down to the cottage in Sussex, but she hadn't wanted to believe it. She had hoped that she might be wrong.

This cheered me a little. That she had been a party to the error of stringing along the affair after its natural demise removed some of the blame from my shoulders. The fact that she had gone on loving escaped me.

'We were both fools,' I said.

'I need help,' she said.

'Well, I've offered to help.'

'You've offered to pay for an abortion.'

'Well, lots of people have it done. It's a simple operation. You're out in a couple of days.'

She said, 'But it's murder, isn't it? It's taking a life. It's already alive. It's a person. They kill it when they drag it out. I couldn't bear to have someone do that to my child. Well, could you?'

The way she put it turned my stomach. At the same time a hard knot of resentment formed in me at the way she insisted on talking about *my* child.

'I take it your father wants you to go through with it,' I said.

'He's a doctor. His job is to save and preserve life.'

69

It sounded pious, but it was irrefutable.

'And what does he expect me to do?'

'He expects us to get married, of course.'

'Of course!' I put sarcasm into it.

She was silent for a time, seeming preoccupied with burning holes in a screwed-up bit of cellophane in the ashtray on the floor with the end of her cigarette. Suddenly she looked up and her eyes were full of tears.

'Is it such a terrible prospect?' she said.

I was going to say, 'It's a bloody impossible prospect,' but there flitted across her face for a moment an expression that took me back, reminded me of the innocent, trusting and adoring Carol of three months before. I felt suddenly tender towards her.

'It wouldn't work, Carol,' I said. 'I mean, marriage is supposed to be for life, isn't it? I know myself too well. I wouldn't be capable of that sort of commitment.'

A tear escaped and she quickly brushed it off her cheek. She said, 'So what are you going to do?'

The confusion of my feelings quite choked me up. I wished more than anything that I could speak out clearly and with assurance and take the situation in hand. I felt that the poverty and shabbiness of my feelings reduced me to a dumb nothing. Perplexed, defeated, self-pitying and suspicious, I was Sartrean man, my self-image distorted, destroyed by the gaze of the other. Her eyes were full of hurt and reproach. We must base our philosophy on peak experience, Colin had said. That was good and true, and philosophy was all very well, but life raised moral problems more thorny than being caught looking through a keyhole.

Bill was delighted to see me back. I had come at the right time, he said. The new project that he'd hinted at some time before but had kept everyone in the dark about was ready to be announced to the world. He had launched a new political party. The *Standard* had carried a paragraph about it the night before, the *Sketch* had picked up the story and given it five column inches, and he had just had both the *Mail* and the *Chronicle* on the phone.

'The Spartacans are going to be big news tomorrow,' he said.

Tom explained. 'Spartacus was a character who raised a rebel army of slaves against the Roman Empire and got himself and most of his followers hacked to pieces. Bill would insist on the name. I think he must have a political death-wish.'

'Don't give us that Freudian crap, Tom,' Bill said. 'I grant you Spartacus was a bad strategist, but he led a revolt against the greatest political and military power the world has known and he damn near brought it off. That's why he's our man.'

'Isn't he a bit obscure?' I said.

'Fabius was obscure to the great unlettered British public, but that didn't stop the Fabian Society making its mark,' Bill said.

Tom chuckled and said, 'It didn't help either.'

Bill rode it. 'Basically, you're right, Tom. There's nothing in a name.'

'A fanatic by any other name would smell as foul,' Tom declaimed.

'There you're wrong, Tom.' Bill took him up seriously. 'Fanaticism is what we need today. Public life in England shows all the signs of a democracy in decline: shameless materialism and cynicism, class antagonisms, lack of vision. We need to make a clean sweep and a fresh start under new men; selfless men, men of vision; in short, fanatics.'

Tom held an imaginary microphone in front of Bill's face and said in the manner of an interviewer, 'And what, Mr Hopkins, will be your first act as Great Dictator, I mean, as Prime Minister?'

Bill said, 'My first act, Tom, will be to line up all cynical, reactionary bastards like you and have you mown down,' and he laughed.

'I see I shall have to start my own party,' Tom said. 'How's that for a slogan: "Cynical Reactionary Bastards of the World Unite!"'

'Lousy!' Bill said, and grimaced.

He had given my name to the papers as one of the founder members of the Spartacan Society. I protested that he shouldn't have done so without consulting me.

'You might not have agreed,' he said. 'Writers are inclined to be so pussyfooting where politics are concerned. I've put Col's name in too, as he'll find out when he reads tomorrow's papers! People like you and Col have to be press-ganged.'

'Yes,' Tom said with a laugh, 'and what a formidable bloody Press Gang it is: William Hickey, Paul Tanfield, In London Last

Night! You don't stand a chance against that gang, Stuart. You'd better submit with good grace and join the ranks!'

The project turned out to be more interesting than I at first thought. Bill had been negotiating with a publisher to bring out at regular intervals volumes of *Spartacan Essays*. He reckoned that with the names Bill gave him as potential contributors he could probably sell five to ten thousand copies of each volume. It would mean a regular income from royalties and—more important—a platform for our ideas. Could I afford to opt out?

'It depends what you mean by "our ideas" Bill,' I said.

'I mean exactly what I say: your ideas, mine, Colin's. We've got to get together and hammer out policies. In England today there's no public debate of the real issues. The important questions aren't even being asked, much less discussed. The job of the Spartacans will be to bring them into the open. We shall be the intellectual power house of this society.'

This was the beginning of a discussion that went on for weeks. Some time before, no doubt, I would have participated in Bill's plans with more enthusiasm, but at this particular time I felt that, with my own house in such palpable disorder, it would be presumptuous of me to try to set the world to rights.

'It seems to me that you've lost your nerve,' Bill said once.

I thought he could well be right, but I argued. 'I haven't, I just don't think that I've got anything useful or original to say on political subjects. And I've no desire to exercise political power. I think this century has had enough of demagogues and ideologies.'

'You sound like one of the gentle anarchists of Dollis Hill,' Bill said. 'That's the politics of the nursery: keep your nose clean and don't have anything to do with strangers. It's not good enough, Stuart. We've got to be committed.'

'To what? People like you, Colin and I are *déracinés*. We have no class interests to defend or promote.'

'Precisely, and that's our strength. Class-based politicians are always fighting today's battles in terms of yesterday's victories. Our commitment is to the future. And I tell you, we'll get a following. People are fed up with politicians who try to capitalise on the old and crumbling antagonisms between the privileged and underprivileged, the boss class and working class. They want vision, ideas, leadership.'

It was the Spartacan publicity that earned us the 'fascist' tag. Journalists and fellow writers with leanings to the left regarded the Spartacans as a sinister symptom, and there was talk of the danger of the younger generation's disenchantment with democracy. As Bill predicted, we gained a following. Private and public meetings were held, discussions and lectures organised, and before long the Spartacan Society was able to boast a nucleus of some forty or fifty members. Bill energetically organised, publicised, proselytised. Colin loyally supported him, though I think he was as sceptical as I was of the value of action on a political front. I remained a fellow-traveller, chiefly out of loyalty to Bill, though I felt all along that my incompetence to handle the problems of my own life disqualified me for any kind of leadership.

'If you're going to break with the Spartacans,' Bill said, 'do it in a few months' time, then we can make it out to be a break over policy. The press will lap it up. Remember the furore caused by Wells's break with the Fabians.'

Of course, Bill and Tom knew about Carol's condition. It made no difference, and little was said about it. It was our problem, not an uncommon problem, and I was grateful to them for being sympathetic, not taking moral attitudes, above all for not saying, 'We told you so.' There was one occasion, though, when Bill came down to my room and after we'd talked about the Spartacan project for a bit he suddenly asked Carol:

'What's going to happen about the baby?'

'What can happen?' Carol said. 'It'll be born.'

'And what about your career as an actress?'

It was a question that hadn't occurred to me, preoccupied as I was with how the problem was going to affect me.

'I'll have to take a year's rest,' she said.

'Then what?' Bill said. 'You can't be out at a theatre every night when you have a young baby to look after, can you?'

'We'll cross that bridge when we come to it,' Carol said firmly. She was, I thought, every bit the brave little woman with brave little clichés, and I felt guilty that nearly everything about her irritated me unreasonably.

'Drop the subject, Bill,' I said. Carol and I had had another harrowing scene that afternoon. 'We've had enough of it today.'

'Speak for yourself,' Carol said. 'It's a relief to me to talk to somebody who can be reasonable about it.'

'Bill can afford to be reasonable,' I said. 'He's not involved.'

'Alright, I won't say any more,' Bill said. 'But you're wrong about my not being involved. When I see two of my friends being the ruin of each other I can't help being involved.'

'You have an overdeveloped sense of the dramatic, Bill,' I said. 'Nobody's being ruined.'

'I hope not,' Bill said, and it was clear from his expression and manner that he reserved his own opinion about that.

Carol and I had had a succession of emotionally wearing and quite inconclusive scenes, but the worst scene of all was the one with her father.

I had met the doctor before, and on that occasion he had taken me to lunch and had confided to me that he considered Carol much improved since she had come up to London. He had even gone so far as to hint that he was fully aware of the real nature of our relationship and quite prepared to connive at it.

But this time there was no offer of a meal, no nod and wink, no man-to-man camaraderie. He came to the house and into my room with as little ceremony as he would have shown had he come in a professional capacity. His manner was brisk and nervous. He ignored my offer of tea and wouldn't sit down. He expressed contempt that I refused to 'do the decent thing' and demanded what I had to say for myself. I said it wasn't myself I was concerned about, but Carol.

'But not concerned enough to marry her.'

'Is concern a good enough basis for marriage?'

'Presumably you felt more than concern when you made her pregnant.'

'I sincerely believed that I loved her.'

That drew his derision. The trouble with my type was that we spent so much time examining ourselves that we didn't know from one minute to the next what we sincerely believed or felt. He supposed that when I'd found out she was pregnant I'd conveniently discovered that I no longer cared for her. I told him it had happened before that, as Carol would confirm. We had virtually separated when I went to Cornwall. I had come back because I wanted to help her.

74

'By getting her to have an abortion? Which is not only dangerous, but illegal too.'

I said I respected her reasons for not wanting to have one. But marriage was out of the question. What would it be for? Just to give the child a name? Surely to marry without love was just to stunt two lives in cringing observance of a social convention, and one that was changing anyway.

Yes, I had all the answers, he said, but one day if I was lucky I'd stop crying for the moon and learn that life only really begins when a man can put himself and his precious freedom in the background and devote his life to someone else.

'Or some*thing* else,' I put in.

The doctor sighed and smiled. 'Yes, I know you writer types fancy that the service of art is the be-all and end-all. But I've done a bit of reading, and it seems to me that all that's worthwhile in literature is an overspill from life. You can choose to shun life and spin your clever webs of words, but they won't add up to anything, believe me.'

It shook me that this little provincial doctor could so precisely formulate my own most secret fears. I saw him suddenly as a man who had had disappointments and disillusions in life, who had perhaps himself experienced the decay of love, but who had in a fashion, and perhaps not so discreditably, come through. But I felt that I still had to fight back.

'You speak as if to avoid marriage is to shun life,' I said.

'I see I misjudged you,' he said. 'I thought you were a mature young man whose influence on Carol could only be for the good. But I was wrong. You've let her down badly, and I'm going to make sure that you don't get away with it scot free. You're going to pay for your mistake, my boy, and if you don't do it willingly we'll slap a paternity suit on you.'

'That won't be necessary,' I said.

'We'll see,' he said.

And I was resolved that it shouldn't be necessary. After this scene with her father I decided that I would stick by Carol and see her through her pregnancy if only to prove him wrong. We reached a kind of accommodation in the weeks that followed. Carol, in fact, was so accommodating that I sometimes suspected that she was engaged in a subtle campaign to gain by stealth what she and her

75

father had failed to gain through emotional or moral coercion, that she was demonstrating what a good little self-effacing wife she could make. There were no tantrums, no demands, and despite our poverty she acceded without demur to my insistence that she shoud accept no financial help from her father. This was one of the conditions that I laid down for myself so that I might extricate myself eventually with as much honour and self-respect as possible. Another condition—but one that I kept to myself—was that I shouldn't sleep with her. I took to working late into the night in the spare room. This, too, Carol accepted without complaint or even comment. Things might have gone on in this way indefinitely but for the new sequence of events that began at one of the Spartacan meetings.

Oliver Moxon's spacious Belgravia house seemed an oddly inappropriate setting for a meeting of a subversive political society. Everything about it proclaimed a vested interest in the class-structured, privilege-ridden order of society that the Spartacan philosophy, as Bill expounded it, regarded as a brake on the advancement and effectiveness of the man of genius and vision. But Oliver himself was quite a catch for the Spartacan movement with his wealth and political experience, which, though it didn't go beyond the hustings, was more than any other founder Spartacan could boast of. He had stood as a Liberal candidate in parliamentary elections, and his politics, he declared, were those of Edmund Burke, but Bill had persuaded him that there was room for all shades of opinion within the Spartacan movement.

About fifty people had gathered for this particular meeting, which Colin was to address. The room was packed and a lot of us had to sit on the floor. I knew about half the people there and recognised several of Bill's recent catches—a septuagenarian titled lady, a pretty actress, a publisher—and several writers and journalists, and there were others whom I couldn't place although their faces were familiar. Among these was a young woman sitting across the room talking to a young man dressed rather conspicuously in a plain respectable business suit. I racked my brain to place her, but unsuccessfully.

Suddenly Bill was standing before the assembly with his arms outstretched above him, as if he were offering himself as a candidate for crucifixion or acknowledging the roar of a crowd after a boxing triumph. This gesture achieved the intended effect of reducing the loud hubbub of conversation to a low murmur, above which the autocratic contralto of the elderly titled lady rang out, firmly putting an American in his place by telling him that she was 'irreconcilably against the pillaging of Britain's cultural treasures by barbarian New World entrepreneurs armed with their ridiculous almighty dollar'. Her point made, she gave Bill a sweet smile and her undivided attention. He proceeded to introduce Colin, thanking him for coming up from Cornwall and greeting him with a vigorous pumping of the hand and a slap on the shoulder as befitted a meeting between comradely giants. Colin, his tall, rangy figure dressed as usual in a bulky fisherman's jersey and baggy trousers, smiled boyishly and nodded to his audience. He started to talk about an American psychological researcher who had conducted experiments with rats and proved that only five per cent had leadership qualities and without them the rest became malleable and completely without initiative. The same applied to human beings, he said, as had been proved by the behaviour of American prisoners subjected to Chinese 'thought reform' techniques during the Korean war.

I suddenly remembered where I had met the girl before. It was the expression on her face as she listened that reminded me. She had worn the same expression listening to the conversation of the brothers, Paul and Brian. It all came back, the looks we had exchanged, the kiss in the wild garden, the feel of her rough hands. It seemed long ago, with all that had happened in the interim, but it was only a few weeks. I wondered what she was doing here, and who the smiling tailor's dummy beside her was.

The implications were inescapable, Colin said. The effective political power ought to be in the hands of the five per cent minority who were equipped to use it, and it wouldn't be while political advancement depended on class or party loyalties. Changes only came about in the world because they were engineered by men of vision, men with ideals. The superior man, the most highly developed human being, was the one who was continually setting himself goals to aim at, and the same applied to a society. The best and highest form of society was the one that was continually evolving beyond itself. Which raised the question of religion. A new and

77

dynamic society must have a new and dynamic religion, a religion that specified a purpose both for the individual life and for that of the society.

The point was taken up in the discussion that followed Colin's talk, and someone suggested that 'dynamic evolutionism' should be adopted as the official religion of the Spartacan movement.

'I can't see it ever being a rallying call for the masses,' our host said.

'We're not concerned with rallying the masses,' Bill said. 'We're concerned with leading them.'

When the meeting broke up I went over to where Sue Rowland was standing. 'Hello, how's Sussex?' I said, and she answered as inanely, 'Oh, it's still there, or at least it was this morning when we left,' but I knew from her expression that she too remembered the events of our previous meeting.

She introduced her friend as James Warren, 'my escort'.

Bill had met the brothers and Sue on a visit to Sussex with Paul, and he suggested after the meeting that Sue and James should join us back at the house for a drink. Several of us piled into James's large white Vauxhall to drive back.

'Well, are you converted, Sue?' Bill asked her in the car.

Sue laughed. 'Whatever to?'

'Spartacanism, of course.'

'No, Bill,' she said. 'But don't let it worry you. After all, I'm only a woman.'

'One thing I deplore,' Bill said, 'is people who parade their misfortunes as excuses for intellectual flaccidity. You can't help being a woman, Sue, but you can help not having opinions.'

Sue was unimpressed by the epigrammatic weight of the reproach. 'I do have opinions, Bill,' she said, 'but I don't always want to air them.'

'God, if Mrs Pankhurst could hear you she'd turn in her grave.'

'I think it must have been rather fun to be a suffragette,' Sue said gaily, 'and to have all those pompous gentlemen running rings round themselves and getting apopleptic.'

'Arguing with a woman is like grappling with smoke,' Bill said.

On his occasional visits to London, Colin was indefatigably exuberant and sociable. If you were anywhere in his path you got swept up in a non-stop round of parties, social visits and sessions in pubs and clubs that demanded a high degree of physical, intellectual and alcoholic endurance. Quite unwittingly and unassumingly he took over the house. He bought lots of wine and poured it liberally for anyone who happened to be around. So on this occasion there was soon a very merry and convivial party scene in progress. The conversation ranged widely, there was a lot of laughter and amiable raillery, and Colin, sprawled at his ease on Tom's bed, sipping a tumbler of red wine, exuding satisfaction and enjoyment, in the course of conversation came out with one of his more outrageous opinions: that all mental patients ought to be shot.

Sue had said nothing up to this point. She had just sat on the floor, listened, laughed, sipped wine, and appeared to be enjoying the occasion. But now she rose as if to a personal challenge.

'That's an incredible and frightening statement, Colin,' she said. 'I worked in a mental hospital for six months and if you had done the same you might have a right to talk about mental patients, but I assure you you wouldn't hold the same opinions.'

Colin said he hadn't the time to try it, but he was sure it wouldn't change his opinions in the least.

'You should make time,' Sue said. 'You'd be surprised. You'd meet some very highly evolved people there.'

Now provoked, she had more to say. Colin's statement about mental patients was typical and showed up a basic flaw in 'dynamic evolutionism'. There was no love or compassion in it. It was cold, arid and inhuman.

Bill recalled the conference we had attended on 'The Quest for Meaning', and remarked that mediocrities always tended to come to the half-baked conclusion that love was the answer to everything. That was the basis of Christianity, which in two thousand years had only succeeded in getting the world into a hell of a mess.

I wanted to dissociate myself from Colin's and Bill's extremism. I reminded Bill that I had agreed with what was said at the conference, but had said at the time that just to express a pious belief in love was no answer to anyone's problems. I said I agreed with Sue that a social or religious philosophy lacking love and compassion was arid. 'But really to love is demanding work,' I said. 'Yes, evolutionary work. Love isn't a cosy state to settle back in. It's an opportunity. And failure in love is failure in life.'

That proved a conversation-stopper. My friends recognised the confessional note and were momentarily embarrassed. Carol's expression, I noticed, was one of surprise.

Sue and James paid several visits to the house in the weeks that followed. I gathered that she and Brian had separated, Brian had come to London to work and she was living with her mother and baby in Battle. James, her 'escort' as she always called him, was an old friend who was on leave from a job in Africa. I wondered if they were lovers, and the more I saw them together the more sure I became that they were not. For one thing, she seemed to reserve the right, in his presence, to be mildly flirtatious with other men, and particularly with me. It was a custom among our group to greet and take leave of female visitors with a kiss on the cheek—a little touch of self-assertive gallantry that Bill had initiated—and whenever Sue offered me her cheek it seemed to me that she did so more coquettishly and lingeringly than she did to the others. She accompanied it with a little inclination of her body towards me which made me sharply aware of parts of her as exquisitely moulded but more fully fleshed than the high and gently curved cheekbone just below which I placed my kiss, and at the same time she gave me a look that maddened me, for I was at a loss whether to construe it as complicity in the desire she aroused or mockery of it.

'Have you been having an affair with that woman?' Carol asked one night after such a little scene. And 'I wouldn't blame you if you had,' she said. 'I wouldn't even mind. I don't expect you to live an entirely celibate life.'

I hadn't been doing so, in fact. I had followed up Colin's suggestion and resumed my affair with Caroline, the 'nice accommodating, undemanding girl who understands the needs of a man of genius', as he had described her on our walk from Mevagissey to Gorran. I had spent several nights at her flat in Putney. With Caroline sex was simple, joyful and guilt-free. She knew about Carol and about my pact with myself, and she was warm and sympathetic. It helped.

But on this occasion with Carol I forgot my pact, or chose to ignore it, or lacked the strength of will to observe it. Anyway, however it came about, we made love. There had been the talk about Sue, then about my supposed celibacy, and then Carol confessed to feeling frustrated and said that it seemed a shame not to take advantage of the months when she couldn't get pregnant. We had, after all, come to an understanding about the baby and she had accepted that we weren't going to get married. But did I have to keep aloof, be so distant and merely dutiful? I thought she was rather humiliating herself talking like this and I made love to her because in the circumstances I felt that it could be an isolated act with no strings attached, a mutual relief and pleasure as it was with Caroline.

But the simplicities of the night disappeared with the coming of day. The logic, both mine and hers, no longer resolved itself in a cosy complicity. It ran up against dead ends, tangled itself in the *non sequiturs* of the heart.

'I can't help still being in love with you,' Carol said.

The way things had been going before she would never have ventured such a confession, a confession which, I realised, made nonsense of my version of what had happened the night before. She had not used me as I had used her. I had made the mistake of thinking that her need for sex was like my need, a need to alleviate a kind of cramp. That she was a woman, that she was pregnant, and that I was the father of the child in her womb, were facts that I had blindly set no store by. It was not she that should have felt humiliated but I, for she had done it with love.

Pregnancy had changed her. There was a new gaiety and bravura in her manner, a lightness and vigour in her movements, a confidence in her speech.

'I'm worried for you, Stuart,' she said. 'I'm worried what this is going to do to you.'

That was ironical. I laughed. 'Do to me? But you're the one who's going through it. You needn't spare any of your sympathy for me.'

She was wide-eyed, earnest, soft-spoken. 'I don't think I'm the only one going through it. I think you are too, even if you won't admit it even to yourself. In fact I think it might even be worse for you, because I still love you and that helps. And it's because I love you that I want you to gain something from this, which you won't do by shutting yourself off, grudgingly doing what you imagine to be the right thing, and just biding your time until I'm out of your hair.'

Pregnancy was supposed to make a woman cow-like and of-the-earth-earthy, not intuitive and articulate. I was a little awed by this new Carol. I wanted to take her up on the word 'grudgingly', but didn't because in the circumstances it would be a mere cavil.

'Don't you know what to make of me?' she said when I didn't reply. 'Do you suspect I'm just a cunning female? For what it's worth, I promise you I'm not. It's you I'm thinking of, not myself. You only have to accept the fact that you're going to be a father. That's all I ask. It isn't much. You don't have to marry me, or even support me. Just live it through, really live it, and don't shut yourself off and get embittered.'

Her words sank in, but they couldn't change anything. How did one accept the fact that one was going to be a father? A woman, with the creature growing in her, might well go through a spiritual change parallel with the physical one, but I doubted whether a man, even when he was in love with the woman and wanted the child, ever got such joy or satisfaction out of impending fatherhood as a woman did out of motherhood. 'That's all I ask,' Carol had said. 'It's not much.' But what was for her 'not much' was for me impossible, and the demand only drove me deeper into sullen and resentful introspection.

I went with her to the hospital and sat for over an hour on a hard, uncomfortable chair in a bleak and dimly-lit waiting annexe in an out-patients department. At first I sat where I could command a view of the ante-room where about a dozen women were waiting to be summoned into the doctor's or gynaecologist's presence, but then an elderly nurse who looked as if she had had her faced starched as well as her uniform asked me to move, 'because some of the girls get embarrassed'. The implication was that I had chosen that seat in order to indulge in a bit of cheap voyeurism, as perhaps I had, though there was nothing to see out of the ordinary, except occasionally a woman quite decently wrapped in a dressing-gown. If I was stealing a view of anything in that ante-room, it was of an exclusively female world that at one and the same time fascinated and repelled me. They were all presumably strangers to one another, and yet most of them were talking quite animatedly. Carol, I noticed before I was moved by the starched nurse, was as communicative as any of them, laughing and talking with her neighbour. What about? I wondered. 'You'd be surprised,' she said coyly, when I asked her afterwards. 'Obstetrics and men,' I conjectured, and she said 'Maybe' in a tone that really conceded that I was right; but what was surprising was not *what* they were talking about, but the manner, the animation, the lack of social inhibitions. I supposed it to be a kind of comradeship in misfortune.

One thing that struck me forcibly in that hospital as I watched the women going in and out of the ante-room was how dowdy and ugly most of them were and how by comparison Carol shone. Some of them seemed so grotesque that I couldn't imagine how they had got into the condition they were in, or what their men must be like. Carol, of course, wasn't yet very far gone—she was still capable of wearing a belted skirt with a short-sleeved summer blouse and high-heeled shoes—but it was clear that even in the very last stages of her pregnancy she would not look anything like any of these horrors. Seeing her there among the others in the ante-room, chatting away happily in a female world and looking attractive and clearly differing from the others in that she took some pride in her appearance, I quite warmed to her.

Another little incident while I was waiting in that hospital affected me deeply. There was a little old lady in a shabby long black coat waiting there too, and after a while a young ambulance man—he couldn't have been out of his twenties—came to collect her. 'Come into my arms, you bundle of charms', he said as he approached her with open arms; and then as he helped her to her feet: 'What are you doing in this place, then, love? Been a naughty girl, have you?' The old woman—she must have been pushing eighty—chortled as she dragged slowly to the door with the ambulanceman's help. 'Come on, love, I'll race you to the ambulance,' he said, and she chortled again and said something I couldn't catch in a quavering voice. The scene affected me because I felt by contrast with that young man my own emotional bankruptcy. His sympathies could reach out to an old bag of bones, but mine were all knotted up with guilt and resentment and couldn't even extend to the girl I had not long ago regarded as my first and only love.

'You know that everyone will say you're running away, don't you?' Bill said some days later when I told him that I had to get out of London.

'I can't worry about what people say,' I said. 'I'm stifled here. I can't work, I can't even think consecutively. I've got to get away to some place where I can write. I'll be able to earn some money with articles and reviews. I'll be more use to Carol than I am here.'

'Where will you go?'

'I phoned Paul Rowland. His cottage is free.'

Bill looked at me quizzically. 'You know, of course, that James flew off to South Africa a couple of days ago?'

'No,' I said. 'So what?'

'I just thought the fact might have influenced your decision.'

'Look, Bill,' I said, 'don't you think I've got enough on my plate?'

'Too damn much,' Bill said. 'I don't know why you don't simplify your life, marry Carol, and settle down to doing some serious writing.'

'But I'm not in love with Carol,' I said.

Bill was unimpressed. He shrugged. 'Being "in love", anyway, only dissipates one's energies. We've got to change this age, Stuart. That's the only thing that matters.'

'I can't live with a woman I don't love,' I said.

'You're a lousy romantic,' Bill said. 'Have you told Carol?'

'No, I'm going to this evening.'

When I told her she remained composed at first. It was as if it came as no surprise. Only when I raised the subject of money did she become animated. I had proposed to give her half of the small amount that I had in my bank account.

'Oh no, I'm not going to give you that kind of satisfaction,' Carol said.

'What do you mean? What satisfaction?' I said, mystified.

'The satisfaction of being able to salve your conscience by paying out some money.'

'I'm offering to help you, to make things easier for you,' I said with heavy patience. 'It has nothing to do with my conscience.'

'Oh, hasn't it?' she said, knowing better. 'Perhaps you believe that, but I certainly don't.'

'So you're going to refuse the money, hoping that it'll make me feel a heel?'

'I don't know what you'll feel. I really can't concern myself with your feelings. I've got enough to do coping with my own. I refuse the money because I don't want charity; it's the last thing I need.'

Charity, *caritas*, love: it was the one thing she needed, I thought, and the one thing I was quite incapable of giving her. But I kept

84

my pedantry to myself and merely said, 'But it's not charity. I *want* to help.'

'You have to face it. *You can't help.* And I have to face the fact that I'm on my own.'

'We don't have to be at loggerheads,' I said. 'You talk of facing things: well, as I see it, what we both have to face is the situation as it is. I know too well that I can't help in the way you really need help. But you can't deny that having money would make things a bit easier. You seem bent on making a martyr of yourself and a villain of me. It's not necessary. Be reasonable, Carol!'

'Not necessary! reasonable!' Carol repeated with a drawn-out scornful inflection. 'I tell you, your conscience is your own concern. So far as I'm concerned, your attempted kindnesses are even more destructive than your deliberate cruelties. Why don't you behave in character? Why don't you just get on with your own life and leave me to get on with mine? It's what you really want, isn't it? And it would be kinder to me.'

So I went. I dragged my rucksack down from the top of the wardrobe and stuffed in my few clothes and some books. I banged about, left drawers open, cursed when I couldn't find things. Carol's eyes followed my every movement, and I couldn't read the expression in them. Was it mockery, triumph, reproach? Was she awed at what she had done, or gratified that she had forced my hand? Doubt as to what was in her mind, and fear that at the last moment she would break down and create a scene—for now I wanted nothing more than to get away, to find a refuge from these wearing emotional scenes—speeded my packing. Soon I was ready. I hitched my rucksack onto my shoulder and went to the door. Still she didn't move or say anything. I nodded, said briskly, 'See you, then,' and left the room.

At Charing Cross I had second thoughts and went into a phone-box, but I checked the impulse. After all, I thought, perhaps she was right, perhaps it really was kinder to leave her to work out her own life when there was so little I could do for her. I reckoned that she had been stupidly obdurate about the money, though.

4

We had had a succession of still, cloudless days since April. This was 1959, the summer that broke all records, and the Prime Minister, with a General Election coming up in the autumn, beamed confidently and told the nation that they had 'never had it so good', as if the long-standing liaison between the Tory party and the Church of England gave him personal access to the ear of the Almighty and had enabled him to fix up this freak summer for election year.

In London the heat and the stillness were stifling, oppressive and enervating. The fact added a little to my sense of guilt at leaving Carol. But only a little and not for long. London and Carol seemed very far away, and for the first day I gave myself over to feline indulgence in the pleasures of sun and euphoria.

In London I had forgotten the sense of affinity I had with this place and the satisfactions it afforded. Except for the climbing roses and honeysuckle round the walls, the cottage was unchanged since the autumn; inside, the distinctive cottage smell of wood-smoke and paraffin fumes still lingered, though no one had been there for weeks. But outside much was changed; late autumn starkness had given way to summer lushness. The foliage in the surrounding woods was dense, and bird life was loud and multitudinous. Despite the long drought the nearby stream, which came from a prolific spring, still flowed strongly, and its incessant rush and chatter was the only sound to be heard in the still night after the loud rooks in the copse at the top of the hill had finally settled.

I spent those first days reading and my reading was consonant with the mood of the place and served to sustain and deepen a sense of having got back to fundamentals. In the cottage there was a collection of the old blue-backed Oxford editions of standard authors. I re-read Milton, Swift, Wordsworth and Coleridge, and found both a tonic for my senses and meat for my intellect in their measured cadences, their robust polemic and grave reflections. Their sanities were one with the sanities of nature. Coleridge, particularly, spoke to my condition, especially his 'Ode to Dejection' and the lines:

> Joy, Lady! is the spirit and the power
> Which, wedding Nature to us, gives in dower
> A new earth and a new heaven
> Undreamt of by the sensual and the proud.

I had been dejected, had been so far down that I had sometimes doubted that I would ever rise again. And deep down I suspected that my coming to the country was an ignoble escape, that my ability to make such an abrupt transition from life-annulling misery to irrational and carefree contentment proved only an ingrained and unsurmountable superficiality of character. Coleridge's lines, themselves the product of a period of blackest dejection, confirmed my feeling that nature was not a haven of anchorage for the defeated; it was relevant; and joy, irrational happiness, was more than relevant, was the key that gave entry into a new life and a new vision. I chose to ignore the bit about sensuality and pride being disqualifiers.

Commerce with the eloquent and mighty dead was all very well and very satisfying and healing, but it wasn't, strictly speaking, work, and I felt that to justify my retreat I ought to be earning some money to help Carol. I tried to get on with *The Dialectics of Despair*, but found that I had lost the certainties that underlay this ambitious project. Perhaps Bill had been right when he had said that I had lost my nerve. I had lost even the certainty that despair could be tackled as a 'problem'. It seemed now rather that it was an inalienable condition of mature human life, that its forms and causes were too many and too personal to yield a solution to analysis and precept, that each man had to find his own solution, had to 'work out his salvation with diligence'. It was, perhaps, a gain in maturity, but what, I wondered, was the use of maturity if it brought with it a loss of ability to do any work in the world? Better to be illuded and still creative than disillusioned and sterile.

But that suggested an alternative theme. I turned it over in my mind and found a title: *Method in his Madness: an Essay on 'Contemporary Man'*. It would be a study of the manifold and ingenious ways in which men deceive themselves into believing that they live purposefully, a study of political and religious neurosis, done with a sort of Swiftian irony. The epigraph for the book could be taken from *A Tale of a Tub*: 'Happiness is a perpetual possession of being well deceived.' The irony would hinge on the fact that the book would be a *justification* of self-deception. It would confound the sombre Sartrean indictment of 'bad faith' by demonstrating that in order to keep faith with life one often had to break faith with the principles of intellectual consistency and order that the philosopher held so dear. Yes, there was potential in the idea, and just thinking about it gave me back some of the buoyancy I had lately lost. Who had said that the existentialists wrote philosophy in the manner of a thriller? Well, I would write it in the manner of a comedy. Sartre and Camus, the prevailing European literary colossi, had not had the last word. They might yet have to cede their laurels.

It was nearly a week after I had arrived at the cottage that I first called on Sue Rowland in Battle. A shaggy and exuberant Welsh collie announced my arrival. It kept ahead of me, barking, all the way up the winding, overgrown path to the bungalow. Sue answered the door. She had on a short blue kimono with a sash knotted at the waist. She greeted me cordially, with unaffected pleasure and no hint of embarrassment.

'We're sunbathing in the garden,' she said. 'Do come through.'

The bungalow was shabby; not shabby-genteel as one might have expected of the home of former colonials fallen on hard times, but unrepentantly shabby. The garden was even more of a jungle than it had been the last time I visited, the accessible part of it consisting of a small clearing of rough grass outside the French windows.

'This is our sun-trap,' Sue said. 'Fetch one of those wicker chairs from the sitting-room. You're just in time for tea.' When she learned that I had come down the previous weekend she said with mock reproach, 'You mean to say you've been at the cottage all this time and didn't come to see us?' The 'us' associated her mother, who was sitting in a deck chair shaded by a large parasol, with the alleged slight. I didn't know whether to feel flattered or disconcerted to be regarded as a friend of the family. From the start she had me off balance.

88

'I've been working hard,' I said. In fact, I had resolved not to rush over to see Sue as soon as I got down to the country. I didn't want to give anyone, even myself, grounds to suspect that her being around had anything to do with my decision to come. I wouldn't go so far as to claim that I had renounced philandering, but I had certainly learned to be more cautious and less opportunistic in affairs of the heart.

Sue, too, was cautious. On her visits to London she had been blatantly flirtatious, but not so now.

(*'In London there were always other people about,' she explained later. 'I could flirt with impunity. But it's quite a different matter when you're alone with someone. And you had a terrible reputation, you know.'*)

Her mother was a grey-haired woman of about fifty who had retained a youthful figure and good looks. She had a fey, not-quite-of-this-world manner, and she talked about life in India before Partition.

'This summer weather takes one back. That was the good life. You had servants, sumptuous clubs, tennis tournaments, splendid balls, and you never even saw anything so gross as a dirty nappy. And now look what I've come down to! At my age!'

Her laugh took the self-pity out of it, made it a quite jolly reflection on one of life's little ironies.

'Go on,' Sue said, 'you had it so good for so long, it's only right that you should have a taste of the harsh realities. You know' —she turned to me—'we hardly ever saw our mother. She was a glamorous creature in a ball-gown who came to kiss us goodnight when we'd been put to bed and floated out on a perfumed cloud. It probably has something to do with why we get on so well now.'

Sue, as a mother, seemed to apply the lessons of her own up-bringing. She was capable but unfussy. While she lay on the grass her child, who had just reached the perilous biped stage, made heavy work of foraging for daisy and dandelion heads with which to adorn her hair. Sue attended to the child's needs, comforted him when he fell or stung himself on a nettle, briskly whisked him away and cleaned him up when a sagging nappy announced the recent performance of an act of incontinence, and bore his crude attempts at floral arrangement with easy insouciance.

89

We spent the afternoon in conversation and there were no under-tones or indications from Sue that she regarded me otherwise than as an acquaintance from London who had dropped in. She had shed her kimono to sunbathe. She lay on a rug wearing a brief bikini and was gay and chatty and quite unsexual, and I wondered how she and her mother would react if I were to act on an impulse to lie beside her and take her in my arms.

(*You looked at me in such a frank, sexually-appraising way,*' she said. '*It made my stomach turn.*'

'*You didn't show it,*' I said. '*You seemed extraordinarily cool.*'

'*I wasn't going to be one of your pushovers. I knew a lot about you from Bill and Tom. So I talked at you and kept you at a distance.*')

She was re-reading *Wuthering Heights* and asked if I didn't think it was a great book. I had to confess I hadn't read it.

'Oh dear, because it's by a woman, I suppose,' she said.

'No, I just haven't got round to it.'

'You should.'

I did. I found an old small-print edition among Paul's books at the cottage and had read it by the time I saw her again. We went for the first of our evening walks and discussed it. Heathcliff, I said, was not really the type of the Byronic hero. His precursors were Milton's Lucifer and Bunyan's Pilgrim. The book was more than a great love story. It had mythic resonance. It was a story of a fall, followed by a pilgrimage and the regaining of Paradise. Sue protested that my reading of the book left out Cathy, who was surely one of the greatest female characters in literature, who was wild, refused to be tamed, and had that marvellous sense of belonging to the moors. She thought that literary people must miss a lot by comparing books with others and reading myths into them. She begged me not to go home and read *Jane Eyre*. We laughed and I promised not to.

There were to be other times like this, when our minds met and clashed and when I recognised in her a quality of mind different from mine, yet no less assured in its values and priorities. I hadn't before come up against a woman who remained so undaunted by my transports of intellection and stuck so firmly by her own view of the matter.

We went for walks almost every evening, deep into the country, far away from any roads. She knew all the tracks and rights of way.

We crossed meadows, climbed fences and gates, wove through dense copses, descended through a chestnut wood to a hidden lake. Sue did most of the talking, following the policy she later confessed to, of keeping me at a distance. She talked about people we knew, about Bill and Tom and her friend James; and about people I didn't know, local eccentrics, her family, her sister who was married to an army officer posted in Germany. Her talk was exuberant and unaffected; people and events came vividly to life in her narration. It was more than a social accomplishment; it showed a talent for life. Her talk, like all else about her, was a novelty to me. It was a novelty that she didn't rigidly demarcate small-talk and big-talk, and could effect the transition from the one to the other, from the level of gossip about people to that of quite sharp and considered observations upon life and ideas, with an ease that demonstrated that life was all one to her and in all its aspects worthy of interest and concern. And her voice was a fine instrument for the expression of the range of her talk, low-pitched, attuned equally to levity and gravity and with a nice control of emphasis, yet quite natural and unaffected.

Gradually I fell more and more under her spell. If she had set out deliberately to make me fall in love with her she couldn't have contrived a subtler or more effective strategy.

(*I didn't exactly set out to do so,*' she said. '*But on the other hand I saw no reason why you shouldn't love me to distraction. I mean, knowing what I did about you, I doubted that you were capable of being hurt by it, and I thought anyway it wouldn't do you any real harm if you were.*')

Our walks usually ended at one of the village pubs, where we drank half pints of cider. On one of our first evenings, sitting at a quiet corner table, Sue told me about the break-up of her marriage.

'It had to happen. I made the mistake of marrying a man much older than myself. As a teenager I was very serious and intolerant, and I regarded most people of my own age as mindless fools. Brian was thirty-nine, gay, intelligent, easy-going, knowledgeable. I was bowled over. But it didn't last; it couldn't with that age-gap. It was all over between us eighteen months ago, before Christopher was born. I'd have left then, but suddenly he fell ill. They suspected T.B. When they told me the treatment and convalescence might last two years, I wept for days. I couldn't walk out on him then, when he was at his lowest and needed me, but also I couldn't bear the thought of two more years out of my life. I wanted to get on with my own life, to get back to living in my own time, among people of my own generation. I'm not a martyr type. I couldn't waste my life paying for a wrong decision I made at twenty.'

'I know how you feel,' I said, and told her about my own marriage and divorce.

'I know,' she said, and the way she said it made me wonder how much else she knew. Neither of us had mentioned Carol, though Sue had of course met her in London.

Sue's recent dilemma, I felt, paralleled my present one, in that she too had refused to mortgage her future to pay for a mistake and had been capable of a certain ruthlessness. But the difference was that she had stuck by her sick husband for eighteen months after it was all over with them. On that account alone, I felt, her sympathy might have very strict limits; and then there was the fact that as a woman, and one who herself had a child, her sympathies might extend equally, if not more, to Carol.

With this undertow of doubt and uncertainty in my mind, I felt safer when our talk was about Sue's life rather than my own.

She told me that before she married she had been halfway through training as an occupational therapist and had worked for some months in a mental hospital. She had had to give it up because she was heading for a breakdown. The work, she said, was both physically and emotionally strenuous. 'And when you're nineteen and fresh out of college armed only with book-learning, and you have to deal with people who are mentally disturbed and can be violent, it's a very taxing job, particularly if you're the type of person, as I was, who tends to identify too much with the patients and kick against the system.'

'Would you think of going back?' I asked her.

'I think I could now. I'm tougher. And I could take up where I left off any time. But I'm certainly not thinking of it for the moment. I've some catching up to do in the matter of just living.'

That was promising. I knew what I would have meant by that, what I had meant when I had proposed a similar programme for myself after the break-up of my own marriage. But then she said:

'Germany should be fun.' We were sitting at a corner table in the Chequers in Battle when she first told me that she and her mother were shortly going to spend two months with her sister. My expression must have betrayed my feelings of loss and frustration, for she reached across the table and took my hand and said, 'I'm sorry I didn't tell you before.' It was her first gesture that admitted a degree of intimacy that went beyond just friendship.

('*Considering your reputation,*' *she said, '*I was surprised that you hadn't turned on more pressure sooner. You seemed almost as shy as I was.*'

'*I must have been lulling you into a false sense of security,*' *I said.*

'*I don't think so. I certainly never felt very secure in that sense. Sex was always just below the surface. Even when we were talking quite seriously you sometimes looked at me in a way that stopped me in my tracks. But you were surprisingly slow getting beyond the stage of just looking longingly.*'

'*Yes. In fact it was you who finally took the plunge.*'

She laughed at the memory. '*Yes, I remember thinking to myself, "Hell, we might as well get this over. It's got to come some time!"* ')

This was an occasion when I called in the late afternoon and found her alone. Her father had just returned from Germany to spend some time at home before taking them back, and he and her mother had gone to visit Sue's maternal grandmother in Brighton.

She was sunbathing in the garden again when I arrived. I took off my shirt and lay there too and we drank tea and talked for an hour or so. Then she had to feed Christopher and get him to bed. And when she came back to join me in the sitting-room she still had on the short blue kimono. She said she was afraid she couldn't go out until her parents returned at about nine and if I wanted to go to the pub she'd join me later. I said I wasn't a solitary drinker but would go back to the cottage if she wanted me to.

There was an awkwardness between us. Walking in the country or sitting in a pub, we could more easily keep up the act of being good friends who acknowledged each other's physical attractions, but alone in the house it was more difficult, and by now tensions had built up.

'We'll have a drink here, then,' she said. Her father had brought some duty-free whisky. With evident relief at being able to busy herself with something, she found glasses and a soda-siphon and poured two stiff drinks.

93

'My father encouraged us to drink quite young,' she said. 'He believed that it was a necessary social accomplishment. I remember him saying to me when I was about sixteen, "You must learn to take your drink like a gentleman." He didn't seem to have noticed that I was a girl!'

Laughter eased the tension. She had a fund of comic anecdotes about drunken subalterns at Sandhurst balls, and I was able to reciprocate with a few amusing incidents from my own experience. She poured a second drink and began to talk more seriously, telling me about some of her experiences in the mental hospital. Once she had disregarded the rule that nurses always had to go in pairs at nights and had got herself locked up alone in a small store-room with a potentially violent patient and had had to talk to her soothingly for over an hour before she was missed and rescued. On another occasion, this time in obedience to the rules, she had abruptly left a patient at the sound of an alarm bell which was rung for drill, and the woman had launched herself at and smashed a glass door that Sue had just shut, causing flying glass to cut her face and neck. She pointed out the little white scars she still had on and under her jaw. She told these stories to illustrate how set rules are at once necessary and inadequate in a job in which so much is unpredictable. They awakened in me a feeling of tenderness for her and a thankfulness that she had come through without being seriously hurt.

Soon we had emptied our glasses again and Sue proposed and poured another drink.

'Live dangerously!' she said with a flourish.

I was standing with my back to the fireplace. She came towards me with the drink, but instead of giving it to me she reached over my shoulder and put it on the mantelshelf. Her eyes held mine and I felt her hand close on the back of my head. She rose slightly on her toes and gently drew my head down to meet hers. It was a long and tender kiss, searching and intimate.

'Well, that's got that over,' she said when we came out of it. But her eyes had depths that belied the flippancy of the remark.

Then I kissed her in my way, hard, voraciously, pressing her close, prolonging it. She struggled, succumbed, struggled again.

'I call that living *too* dangerously,' she said afterwards. 'That was more than I bargained for.'

'Didn't your father warn you about that too when you were a little girl?'

'No. Nobody ever told me about people like you. Are there many like you up in Yorkshire?' She had recovered her composure, become humorous and gently mocking.

'I don't know about Yorkshire,' I said. 'I think it's a characteristic of writers. It's a sedentary trade, and one's energies tend to get polarised. They either go to the head or the other place.'

She frowned at the allusion, but then laughed.

(*From the start it was a relationship of mutual mockery,* she said. *You mocked me because I was, as you thought, arrogant and strait-laced, and I mocked you because you had some deplorable ideas and it was obvious that women had always spoiled you terribly.*)

If I hadn't put on the pressure before this incident, I certainly did after it. I kissed her again and she was yielding and ardent, and I began to think that there was time yet before her parents returned for the consummation that my body craved. And when she said, 'I'm dying to spend a penny,' and left the room, I took it that she only meant that there is an order of precedence in the calls of nature, but when she returned she had changed from her kimono into a high-necked dress.

'You were looking at me as if I were something to eat,' she said.

'You are,' I said, 'and I want to make a long, long meal of you.'

'I don't want to be a meal,' she said petulantly.

Months before, in the garden on the first day we met, she had cooled suddenly after, as I thought, leading me on all day with her looks. And now, after so boldly and provokingly taking the initiative, she had abruptly distanced herself. The perversity of woman! I thought. Sue looked embarrassed, discomposed, nervous. This, perhaps she knew, was the age-old predicament of woman: to have to choose between being secretly despised if she too readily gives what is so ardently solicited and being castigated as a callous teaser if she withholds it. She withheld it and I felt she was being perverse because callous teasing would not be in character, and I suspected that perhaps she really was naive about sexual relationships and asked her about her marriage. She was noncommittal, but I gathered that there hadn't been much on that level after the first careless rapture that begot young Chris. Then I asked her about James and she confirmed the impression I had got in London, that he really had been just her escort, but the way she put it now was that James was a 'gentleman'. The way she said that, accompanying it with a little smile, pleased me. It pleased me to think that I stood to gain by brazen northerner's directness what James and a host of Sandhurst subalterns, inhibited by the scruples of their class, had failed to gain by pussyfooting around their idol.

'You're incredibly beautiful,' I said.

'It's in the eyes of the beholder,' she said.

'I love you.'

'You mean you find me sexually attractive.'

'More than that. Isn't it a reciprocal feeling?'

'Can I remind you of something you once said?' She was now very serious.

'What was that?' I said warily.

'It was the evening of that Spartacan meeting I went to. The words stuck in my mind because they struck me at the time as a strange thing for a literary Casanova to say. You said in effect that being in love is only an opportunity, that staying in love is hard work and that "failure in love is failure in life". Do you remember? Or was it just talk?'

'No, it wasn't just talk,' I said. 'I meant it.'

'Then don't you think we had better remain just good friends?' she said. 'It would be a pity to spoil what is, after all, a rather interesting friendship.'

The mood had changed. We had been engaged in a game, a contest, but now Sue had suddenly raised the stakes. On one level I felt aggrieved at the foundering of my erotic expectations, but on another grateful to her for her lucidity and seriousness.

This *entente cordiale* was as provisional and unstable as any political one. The game had just become more complex. Sue had won a round by turning against me my own professed ideals, which accorded with her own, and in future engagements I would now have a formidable weapon in that I knew I could awaken her sensuality. It was, as she said, an interesting friendship, but the chief interest of it lay in the shared knowledge that each expressed in word and action what the other kept suppressed. We continued to play our roles, I the sensualist and she the woman of principle, and to mock in each other what secretly we cherished, but it was all a game now of mutual exploration, a probing of depths, a testing of breaking points. For my part, I was certain that it could have but one outcome, that the interesting friendship stage must lead on to and enrich a full and uninhibited erotic relationship.

(*'I must admit I was sometimes alarmed at the feelings you aroused in me,' she said. 'I might have submitted had I not found myself getting rather fond of you. I sometimes thought it would be interesting to have a nice little harmless affair.'*

'You told me you didn't want to take that memory of me to Germany.'

'Yes, and I suppose what kept me adamant was my pride, together with the fact that, as I say, I was becoming quite fond of you. I wasn't going to be another scalp on your belt. And I was going to Germany soon and expected you to be gone when I got back. I reckoned I could put up with a bit of frustration for the sake of my pride. And anyway it wasn't all frustration. A lot of it was romantic and fun. Do you remember the night of the ridiculous moon?')

Yes. After that evening we had to see each other every day. I would take a bus or thumb a lift into Battle, and after Sue had settled the baby we would go for our walk. We walked for miles across and around the country, sometimes talking, often in silence, just being together, seeing together, sharing a sense of wonder and delight in the world. The perfect summer continued and seemed our private benediction. All that was beautiful or awesome in nature, all growing things and living things, the colours, the movements, the sounds, the scents of summer in the air, were ours. We never tired of watching, listening, being together, pointing out things, telling each other what the world was like. All our senses were awakened and exquisitely sharpened, and the need to be one was not just a need for physical union, though that was always there, but a need also to respond as one, to feel the same feelings, share the same perceptions, to be in every sense and with every sense together in the world. 'Look!' one of us would say, and it might be a splendid sunset or a quicksilver squirrel following an intricate path among high branches. The strange affinity we had with each other was complemented by a shared affinity with the commonplace marvels of the world.

Sometimes we would be like children, racing, hiding or trespassing, and I would leap gates and climb trees and delight in making her worried for my safety. And sometimes I would run ahead of her, sit on the grass and watch her approach, intently watching the way she moved, making her conscious of her body and her movements. My scrutiny embarrassed her and she protested, but she did not let it discompose her; she just walked steadily on and when she came level kept out of my reach, for the first time I had done it I had suddenly lunged and brought her down on the grass beside me. At other times I dropped behind and watched her walking ahead, but for some reason she objected more to this and when she caught me at it she stopped and waited for me to catch up or came back to me. And when we came to a gate I climbed over first and in helping her down held her close and let her body slide slowly down against mine, and kissed her.

One evening we came to a cornfield. It was getting dark, and the grass around was loud with the twittering of settling birds. The path we were on led up a steep incline and at the top a ridge was sharply outlined by a strange brightness beyond. When we reached the ridge we both stopped, breathless, for suddenly we were face to face with an immense harvest moon. It was so low in the sky, so close, so perfectly full and round, so bright and yellow, it was awesome, miraculous, a heavenly visitation consecrating the earth. Below it, just ahead of us, was this field of tall corn, bright yellow too, rustling and waving. We had shared other wonders and delights, but this surpassed all, stirred a wild joy, made us at first speechless, entranced. Then we both laughed, for it was too perfect, almost like a Hollywood scenario, and hand in hand we ran across to the cornfield. I said we should plunge into it, lie there, make love and celebrate the miracle in a thoroughly pagan way, and Sue said it would be terribly prickly and uncomfortable, I should be romantic and woo her with sweet melodies like Nelson Eddy.

'It's an absolutely ridiculous moon,' I said, and she said did I know that anyone who escaped from a mental hospital and remained at liberty for a full moon-cycle was automatically deemed sane? I said she was beautiful but had a mind full of irrelevant facts, which made her pretend to be indignant and she ran away up the hill, but I didn't chase her because it was marvellous to watch her moving, silhouetted against the sky with the moon so low and so close that it seemed she could have run right up to it.

Afterwards we always spoke of the occasion as 'the night of the ridiculous moon'. The incident was typical of the mood of these days. Romantic and impassioned we were, but we had both had experiences that made us wary of such feelings, and we sought through mockery of each other and of our situation to maintain balance and a sense of proportion. We both had private reasons to feel that this was an inappropriate time to be involved in an idyll.

But I found myself experiencing strange and unprecedented feelings. One evening a young man we had met in a pub and whom Sue knew slightly and addressed as 'Malcolm' offered to drive me back to the cottage. He worked in the City and was down for the weekend staying with his parents, who had a farm nearby. From his voice, manner and dress I judged him to be one of the privileged effete, but I accepted the lift and the half bottle of whisky that we all drank back at the cottage. Then came the time when Malcolm had to drive Sue home. I walked up the fields with them to the road and watched until the tail-lights of the car were out of sight and the throaty roar of its engine, which I judged as affected as its owner's voice, had faded into the night. Back at the cottage I lay awake for hours working myself into a stew imagining what Malcolm might have done on the way back. He was the kind of cowardly runt that would get boozily amorous. And Sue would be quite helpless. My imagination ran wild, and I saw myself the next morning striding up the drive of the parental farm, demanding to see their 'gentlemanly' son, and there and then giving him such a pasting that he wouldn't be able to show his face in the City for at least a couple of weeks. I dwelt on the scene with such a sense of savage satisfaction that I eventually alarmed myself with the thought that I was actually wishing for something to have happened so that I could demonstrate to Sue what an ill-bred passionate man I was.

It was a point that didn't really need demonstrating.

(*'I thought you were a strange creature to have suddenly come into my life,' she said. 'I wasn't sure that I really liked you.'*

'You appeared to like me.'

'That wasn't liking, was it? You excited and intrigued me. You were so blatantly sexual. You aroused strange sensations in my body. I thought you had no right to make me feel like that. You took liberties that no one had ever dared take before and I let you because it was

99

strange and exciting, but at the same time I resented my loss of freedom and feared what you would do to me if I succumbed completely.')

Late one night we sat drinking coffee on the floor in her sitting-room by the light of an electric fire. Her parents had been in bed when we got back to the bungalow. We had gone straight to the kitchen to make coffee. I was grinding the beans in a hand-grinder when suddenly I caught her staring at me. She was standing by the wall opposite me waiting for the kettle to boil. We had been touching and kissing all evening and I knew by the way she stood and by the solemnity of her expression that her entire body was awakened. Mine was too. We ached for each other, for closer, deeper union and for the tranquillity that would ensue. She confessed as much, and I turned on the pressure, and she let the process of sexual escalation go further than it had ever gone before, but when I said, 'We must go to your room' she broke away and was so distressed and emotional that I didn't know what to say or do. 'I simply don't understand you,' I said when she had regained her composure.

In the sitting-room, as we sipped coffee in the semi-darkness, she tried to explain.

'It's not that I'm a particularly moral girl, if that's what you think. In fact, once, not long ago, I offered myself to a man.'

I felt a flush of anger and jealousy rise to my face, and my lips involuntarily tightened.

'Does that shock you?'

'It surprises me. Was it James?'

She nodded. 'It was soon after Brian had gone. It had been such a bleak two years. I felt I had some catching up to do. I thought I'd play the old *femme fatale* for a bit. On one of our first trips up to London James and I stayed at a hotel. We had adjoining rooms. I told him he could sleep with me if he wanted to.'

'And he didn't?' She shook her head. 'How ungallant,' I said, but inwardly I seethed with anger and a sense of betrayal. Sue looked calm and thoughtful.

'He said I'd hate him afterwards. He said I was unhappy and not myself and he'd rather wait until I'd got over the break-up of my marriage. For the time being all he wanted was to take me around and give me a good time.'

'Very gentlemanly,' I said. 'It showed remarkable self-control.'

I just managed to get the words out before a constriction seized my throat, tears welled into my eyes and my whole body started trembling. I felt intense pangs of anger, of jealousy, of tenderness for her, of awe at James's behaviour, and of thankfulness for the outcome. There could be no resolution of such a turbulence of conflicting emotions except in tears. Yet I was as surprised as she was at the vehemence of my passion.

'Whatever is the matter?

'I . . . I think I really do love you.'

She laughed and drew my head down and holding it against her breast stroked my brow and cheeks and smiled down at me. 'That's a true philosopher's declaration,' she said.

'I don't know what came over me,' I said. 'I find myself prey to such strange fits of emotion where you're concerned.'

'It's jealousy.'

'Did you aim to make me jealous? Is that why you told me?'

'No. I was explaining. You see, I'm not particularly moral.'

'Then why not try the *femme fatale* bit on me?'

'For two good reasons. First I don't know for sure who it would be fatal for; and second, I know that you'd take me up.'

'And you knew that he wouldn't?'

'Perhaps, deep down, but I couldn't have been sure. He was right when he said that I wasn't myself at the time, and I probably would have hated him and myself afterwards if we'd gone through with it. The trouble is, I can't do anything with just a part of myself. Some people seem to have the enviable ability to split themselves up and live in different parts of themselves at different times. I just can't do that. It's a great disadvantage.'

'And you say you're not moral!'

'I'm not. It's not a matter of principle. My mind doesn't come into it. You know the saying "to have no stomach for something"? Well, that's just it. I may think I want to do something, like going to bed with you for instance, but if my stomach rebels I just can't. It's very annoying. My mind says, "Just think: all that lovely violence going to waste!" But it's no good.'

'Your trouble is that you haven't got a mind,' I said. 'You think with your guts.'

'Thank you!' She pretended to be offended.

I walked the six miles back to the cottage that night, and I felt such vigour in my limbs and such lightness in my head that I could have walked to London. The moon rode high above the sleeping village and above the fields and farms that I passed. The air was still and the night silent except for the occasional hoot of an owl or a rustling in the hedgerow. I felt a wonderful elation. I thought of Sue sleeping in her room with her child in its cot beside her. I would have liked to be there, not to disturb her, but just to watch and stand over her. I would tell her when we next met, 'I take back my philosopher's caution. I no longer think I love you. I just love you, full stop.' It would be a joke, I would say it lightly, but she would know just how much weight it carried. Yes, she would know. In the communications of lovers, it seemed, the laws of nature were confounded; the heavier the content, the lighter the vehicle required to carry it. By contrast with this my first real love, all my earlier romances seemed plodding and rhetorical. There had been too much earnestly declared, too little left unsaid, altogether too much weight, too great an apprehension of the void beneath the words. And what applied to love applied equally to work. Intellect must be gay, must go directly to its mark. Thought must be of the gut, instinctive, precise, direct and unconfutable. Of course, she knew that, she had always known it; and, knowing it, she was wiser than most philosophers. Yet she had seemed quite serious when she had spoken of the 'enviable' ability of people to split themselves up, to separate head and heart, body and mind. That could be irony, but it could be a failure to recognise what in her was exceptional, what in my experience at least was unique. In a time that produced divided people, part people, she was miraculously and wonderfully *whole*. And I would have her whole. This at least I would have in common with gallant, gentlemanly James. I would do her no violence, would do nothing to split her up. But unlike him, I would not let her go.

Soon after this she came over to spend a day with me at the cottage. She brought Chris and a carrier-bag of food in order to cook a meal. I met her off the bus so that I could help her carry things across the fields, and when I hoisted Chris onto my shoulders she said anxiously, 'Do mind you don't slip,' and I knew by the way she looked at me and smiled that it gave her pleasure to see me with her child, and I thought how effortless and natural parenthood was and how absurd it was to make heavy work of it.

When we got to the cottage Sue unpacked her things and immediately began preparing the meal. Chris followed her about and got under her feet and I stood by, watching her.

'You men are useless in the kitchen,' she said; 'why don't you go and amuse each other in the garden? I won't be long.'

So I took the child out and looked at a picture book with him. He happily showed off his monosyllabic knowledge, pointing out 'house', 'bird', 'cow', 'puss'. I took it into my head to try to further the child's education and extend his syllabic range, and tried to teach him to respond to the question. 'What kind of a puss is Christopher?' with the answer, 'An oedi-puss'. Oddly enough, the child seemed to find this amusing, and we were still practising it when Sue came out into the garden.

'What are you doing corrupting my child?' she said. But she was laughing.

We sat on the grass. She raised her face to the sun and closed her eyes. 'It's glorious here on a day like this,' she said. 'I hope you like curry, because that's what you're getting for lunch.'

I said, 'You know, you function very well as a woman.'

'How else should I function?'

'I mean, you carry it all so lightly, being a mother, cooking meals. Most of the women I've known have seemed to be discontented with their lot. They've felt that men have all the advantages. But that doesn't seem to worry you.'

Her wholeness fascinated and puzzled me, for it seemed to exclude so much that I had always valued. I wanted to understand her, but perhaps more than that I wanted to vindicate my masculine way of functioning.

'I enjoy being a woman,' she said.

'Yes, and that's marvellous,' I said. 'But there's a very real sense in which discontent is essential to life.'

'Divine discontent,' she said in a low voice. I thought there was a hint of mockery in it, but I went on, tried to explain what I was getting at. Life, I said, was nothing if it wasn't a process of growing. Living, understood as just biologically functioning wasn't worth the candle. And the same went for merely socially functioning. Men weren't as bound as women to biological and social functions, to such things as child-bearing and home-making. And

103

the very rhythm of woman's life, with its twenty-eight-day cycle like the moon's, bound them inescapably to the earth.

'I see,' Sue said slowly, 'you mean that because women have periods they can't have what you call a spiritual life?'

'I wasn't talking about having periods,' I said. 'I'm saying that the very conditions of a woman's life and the demands made on it are difficult to reconcile with what life is really about, namely, growing, or evolving spiritually. The reason you're such a mystery to me is that you seem to have reconciled the two things so effortlessly.'

'You're wrong,' she said. 'There's no mystery. You see, I've settled for being, as you say, bound to the earth. Anyway, if I had a spiritual life, you wouldn't know, would you?' She stood up. Suddenly there were deserts between us.

'I must go and put on the rice,' she said. 'And why don't you open the wine? We can have a glass before we eat.'

I barred her way into the house.

'Kiss me,' I said.

'No.'

'Why not?'

'Because I don't feel like it at the moment.'

'The stomach rebels?' I tried to make her reciprocate a smile, but she wouldn't.

'Yes. Now will you let me pass?'

I yielded, bleakly aware that I didn't know where her flash-points lay. This wasn't a matter of provocation and teasing that could be resolved by a bit of horseplay over her entering the cottage. Or was it? I didn't know. She was an enigma. But I didn't take the risk. I let her pass and opened the wine.

The strain between us lasted right through the lunch. I felt desolate. The magic had gone out of the day. Yet Sue did nothing that I could reproach her with. She was gay and talkative and for all the world as if nothing had happened. It was I who was sulky and uncommunicative. I was well aware of that, nevertheless in my heart I blamed her. She had withdrawn part of herself, the part that I most valued, that I had come to feel was my own privileged preserve. She busied herself with the food, served it up, spoon-fed Chris from a tin of Heinz baby food, and chatted away just as she might have done in the presence of any casual acquaintance. It was a display of social accomplishment, and as such it riled me; but at the same time I was glad of it, because for both of us to have been sulkily silent would have been worse, would have been sure to lead to an eruption and an ugly scene. Yet her aloofness gave me more pain than any bitter recriminations would have done. I resented in her the nonchalance and pride of her class, the ability to put on a superficial but impenetrable mask of calm and normality while the depths bubbled and seethed. In my head I formulated a verbal frontal assault: 'Alright, you've made your point, you're a complex and independent human being with a mind and a life of your own; now cut out the social chatter and come back to me.' The trouble was I didn't know that it would be relevant. I wasn't sure that it was merely social chatter, that there were any seething depths, that the mask wasn't the face. Her playacting, if such it was, was consummate. It was just possible that I was imagining it all, that she had already forgotten or dismissed whatever I had said that had offended her. The thought afforded no consolation, though. I still felt desolate and distanced.

'It's always seemed to me a great shame that one half of the human race should be cut off from the other,' Sue said. This was later, in the afternoon. Chris had been put down for his afternoon sleep, and we were lying in the garden. The sun blazed high in a clear sky and the only sound was of insects humming and buzzing.

'I don't see that the sexes need be cut off from each other,' I said.

'Nor do I, but they are. It's a sad fact. And I'm not saying that men are wholly to blame. Women are just as prejudice-ridden and cliquey.'

I interpreted this as her way of making it up. I felt that she had come back within reach; perhaps it was the effect of the wine, the good meal, the idyllic afternoon. I said, 'Well, you seemed to be blaming me earlier, judging by the way you froze me off.'

'No,' she said. 'I was just a little disappointed. It was rather unoriginal, wasn't it?' But she leaned over and kissed me lightly on the lips.

'You have a sensual mouth,' she said. 'But sometimes you hold it too tight. When you relax your lips, they have a soft, sensual line.' She traced it with a finger. 'Sometimes in London I had an impulse to kiss you just to make you relax that grim, set expression.'

'You should have done.'

'We were never alone. There wasn't the opportunity.'

'We must make up for lost opportunities.'

But I didn't turn on the pressure as I would have done before. I remembered my resolution to do her no violence, to cherish her wholeness. And I had decided that the time had now come when I must tell her about Carol.

'There's something I want to tell you,' I said.

She watched and waited while I racked my brain for the right words. I was nervous. I couldn't imagine how she would react. But it had to be done.

'I didn't tell you before because—well, because I didn't expect things to get so serious.' I took her hand and fondled it. 'You see, the thing I want you to know—because it's important to me now that between us there should be nothing hidden—is that Carol: perhaps you remember her at the house in London?' Sue nodded slightly. 'Well, Carol is pregnant, and by me.'

Did she already know? She appeared to receive the information quite calmly. I searched her eyes for signs of anger, jealousy, reproach, but there were none. She just looked solemn and composed. She averted her eyes and said in a soft voice, 'I'm glad you told me. But why did you?'

'I wanted you to know. I couldn't keep it to myself, things being as they are between us.'

'What are you going to do?'

'I don't know. Things were complicated enough, but now to make them more so I find myself in love with you.'

She shook her head. 'You mustn't let that complicate it. Anyway, I shall be gone in a week.'

'But you'll be back.'

'Two months is a long time.'

'I'll still love you.'

She smiled. 'I'd take odds against that. Anyway, wouldn't it be better for both of us if you didn't?'

'I don't know. I can't judge of better or worse. I only know that I'm in love with you and I can't bear the thought of it not continuing and developing.'

'It's been an idyll,' she said, 'a summer infatuation. After all, we're both on the rebound. People's emotions in such circumstances are notably unreliable. You'll be cured by the time I get back.'

106

'I don't want to get cured,' I said. 'And I don't regard it as an infatuation.'

'No. Well, we shall see.' Her tone was quiet and resigned. 'I think you should try to get cured, anyway. I'd help you, only I'm afraid that just now my stomach wouldn't let me.'

'That wouldn't cure me. It would make it worse.'

'Oh, I don't know.' Now she was crisp and ironical. 'After all, it's only a physical attraction, isn't it?'

'No, it's more than that. It's something complex, different and precious.'

Sue didn't sustain the ironic note. She changed to the elegiac: 'Perhaps. But if it is, it has come too late, hasn't it?'

And it was in an elegiac mood that we spent our last days together before she went to Germany. She didn't return to the cottage after that day, but we saw each other every evening and went for walks and sat in pubs holding hands. Our mutual physical attraction remained undiminished, though there was no question now of its being consummated. We could scarcely bear to be apart, and when we were together we had to be continually touching, embracing, kissing, or simply holding hands. When physical contact was not possible, we held each other with intense looks.

One day when Sue's mother and I were briefly alone together, she said, 'I could boil your head in oil, Stuart, for making Sue fall in love with you. She was just getting over the distress of her marriage and looking forward to the trip to Germany, and now she mopes about and doesn't show any enthusiasm for going.'

Her voice was so light, level and uninflected that I couldn't tell whether her words constituted a genuine reproof or just a tease. I muttered that I was equally stricken myself, and she changed the subject. I cherished the information she had given me, however, for it was more than Sue would admit to, and as the time for her departure drew nearer I became hungry for any scrap of evidence that I had a hold on her that would endure. If she was sceptical about my feelings, I was equally so about hers. In Germany she would be back among her own type of people, and I did not doubt that her natural exuberance and gaiety would soon assert themselves. Sue was not the type to brood upon or let her life be disrupted by a passion that offered little hope of a happy issue. Our physical affinity was an extraordinary and exciting thing, an experience without precedent for both of us, but it seemed a slight and unreliable thing to put any hopes on or to match against the process of emotional attrition attendant upon separation and the inevitable impingement of other lives, other responsibilities, other problems. It was too strong an affinity to be denied or suppressed, and during our last days together we gave it rein up to a point, but always there was a melancholy, elegiac undertow. Not only did two months seem an endless time, but it was impossible for either of us to see what life would be like on the other side of it.

'You should go back to London and Carol,' Sue said.

'I shall see her and try to help,' I said, 'but I shall await your return, and I'll be still around when you come back.'

Sue shook her head. 'Why?' she said.

'Because it can't be otherwise. We can't leave it like this.'

We were sitting facing each other in a loud and smoky bar, hands clasped across a wet and littered table and our eyes avidly reading the melancholy and the hope in each other's face. Sue said, 'Stuart, I don't want to be your escape route.'

'It's not that, I promise you,' I said.

'You should go back to Carol,' she said.

'It's impossible. It would be even if there were no chance of our meeting again.'

She seemed to believe me; at least, she was disinclined to press the point further, except to say, rather wearily, 'Maybe. Poor kid, though! Pregnancy isn't any fun, even at the best of times. You must be kind to her.'

'I will,' I said, poignantly aware at that moment, as in the months that followed, of the sad irony that the promise thus solemnly entered into really had nothing to do with Carol, who was to be its beneficiary.

It was through no intervention of Sue's that her father offered me the use of the bungalow while they were away. In fact, the offer came as a surprise both to Sue and her mother as well as to me. Her father was known to them as a taciturn careful man, not given to acts of spontaneous generosity. Nor did he make the offer in a particularly generous spirit; he just said that it would suit him to have the place occupied while they were away instead of standing empty.

I accepted the offer gladly, and on the day of their departure I left the cottage early with my rucksack, hitch-hiked a lift into the village, and accompanied them to the station. There Sue and I discreetly kissed, I promised to write often and to be faithful to her, and she told me not to make any promises. I said that in two months' time I would be waiting on the other platform just across the line there for her return, but she said she wouldn't depend on it. I told her to enjoy herself, but not too much, and to beware of sneaky subalterns, and she told me to work hard and to be sure to get myself 'cured' as soon as possible. I told her that it was heart-less of her to leave me with her scepticism and mockery as a last memory, and she made up for it by placing upon my lips a kiss of inexpressible tenderness. The train came and I helped them with Christopher and with their luggage. Sue remained leaning out of the window as the train drew away. The wind blew her unruly hair all over her face and she kept using her hand alternately to push it back and to wave to me until the train rounded a bend and we lost sight of each other.

Two long months, I thought. Well, I would work hard and try and get my life in order. The only work I had done in the last weeks was a story entitled 'Nostalgia' which expressed my feelings the night when Sue's City friend drove her home and I discovered in myself an extraordinary nostalgia for violence. I re-read the story, and now it seemed flat and banal. Yet I had written it in a frenzy. It was bewildering that feeling was so delusive and trea-cherous a guide in matters of art; and it was a chastening thought that the same might apply in life. The same did apply. The affair with Carol had begun with just such intense feelings and equally promisingly. I was convinced that with Sue everything was and would be different, but it was a conviction based on feeling. Time would tell and the coming months were going to be a crucial test.

5

The first letter I received from Carol when I was at the cottage was brief and showed no trace of the proud and bitter mood I had left her in. I had been able to send her a little money because an American university had paid three hundred dollars for all the notes and typescript of my book, *Emergence from Chaos*. Carol thanked me for the money and said she would keep it until nearer her confinement. For the present, she could support herself quite well, as she had got a job as a waitress. She offered me my room back, saying she realised I had gone to the country because I couldn't work with her sharing the room, and if I wanted it she could move in with a friend she had made at work. She signed off, 'With love always, Carol.' I replied that work was going well, I was glad to be out of London for these summer months and she was welcome to the room for as long as she wished.

In fact I had done little work during these weeks, but there had been some developments which promised well. In April the magazine *Encounter* had published an extract from my book, *Flight and Pursuit*, which had caught the eye of someone in BBC religious broadcasting, and I was invited to write a half-hour television programme. Also, George Devine at the Royal Court Theatre had liked the first two acts of the play I had completed while staying with Colin in Cornwall, and wanted to discuss the third act and the possibility of a production.

I went up to London a few days after Sue had left for Germany, and it soon became clear that rumours about my life in the country had preceded me. This didn't particularly surprise me. Paul Rowland's cottage was one of three within a mile of each other, all of which had been intermittently occupied that summer by people connected with our group.

There was, as usual, a crowd in Tom's room when I arrived. Tom and Bill were there and Colin was up on one of his brief visits, and among the rest there was a girl of eye-catching prettiness whom I hadn't seen before. But there was no sign of Carol.

I walked in on a scene of general hilarity. I put down my rucksack near the door and Tom came across to greet me and drew me into the middle of the room. He introduced the girl to me as Delphine. Her face, oval in shape and made up of small features, wore an expression of permanent naivety and surprise with its high pencilled eyebrows and heavily mascara-ed false lashes.

'So you're the backwoodsman Bill's told me about?' she said.

'Bill's been building you up as a latter-day Thoreau,' Tom said.

Then Colin came up to me, broadly smiling, and suddenly stuffed something down my shirtfront. It was alive. I felt the thing struggling to get out and panic seized me lest it should bite or scratch. Everyone laughed uproariously, except Delphine, who tore at my shirt, ripping some buttons off, and extracted a small, brown, fluffy creature which she clasped to her breast.

'Poor Caesar! You've frightened him,' she admonished Colin.

'I'm sorry, love, I couldn't resist it,' Colin said. 'Here, let me kiss him better.' Pretending to do so, he nuzzled the girl's breast with a boisterous show of lechery. She slapped him on the back of the head and he drew away, laughing.

The creature was a bush-baby. Delphine released it and it leapt from her hand and clung high up on the curtains, an amazing feat for such a small creature. It surveyed the room with a curiously human expression. Delphine said it should be left alone now for a while or it would develop a complex, so everyone sat down and the noise and laughter gradually subsided.

'Been doing much work down there in the country, Stuart?' Bill said.

'Yes, quite a bit,' I said. 'How's your novel coming on?'

Bill screwed up his face in simulation of the agonies of creation. 'Not very well, Stuart old man.' Then, with heavy irony: 'It's all right for you, alone in the country. But I keep getting involved with people, and that plays havoc with the work.'

'You should get away yourself,' I said. 'There's no place like the country for work.'

'So it seems. Fast work!' Bill guffawed and slapped his thigh.

'Stop bitching, you two,' Tom said. He turned to the girl. 'Women are supposed to be bitchy, but they've got nothing on writers. They're all such bloody egotists, the most malicious breed on the face of the earth.'

Colin, now slumped in a deep armchair, joined in. 'It's not malice, Tom. It's concern for each other. We've got to keep each other up to the mark creatively. Now Stuart has a great disadvantage as a writer because he's cursed with romantic good looks and is attractive to women. And he's a randy bugger. For his own sake someone has to keep reminding him that his intellect is the only interesting and important thing about him, and if his friends don't, who will?'

Though this kind of genial slanging was accepted form among us, I knew that Colin meant every word of it, and I felt obscurely that not to argue back would somehow be disloyal to Sue.

'I don't agree, Col,' I said. 'I think that if a man's strong on intellect his efforts should be concentrated on developing other sides of himself to balance it out. Surely the best writing is that which is an expression of the whole man.'

'That's the great humanist fallacy,' Colin said. 'Let me put you right on this, Stuart, because it's important. Remember that line in Browning's *Paracelsus*: "Man is not man as yet"? Well, that was written a hundred years ago, and it's still true. Quite literally, man does not yet exist. Plenty of "whole men" in your sense of the term exist. You meet them everywhere, contented idiots perfectly adjusted to their environment. Those people's lives are so full and they're so proud of the fact and taken up with the business of living fully that they don't stop for a moment to think, to ask the question, What is man's proper element? Do you remember that passage at the beginning of Wells' autobiography where he says that men are striving to become pure creatures of the mind? That's exactly it. Man's element *is* the mind. But Wells was optimistic. Who are these men who are striving to become pure mind? They're not your so-called "whole" men, who have harmoniously developed all sides of themselves so that they can run like a well-oiled machine.'

'They're the fanatics,' Bill put in.

'Yes, in a sense, Bill,' Colin went on, 'but they're not your revolutionary or social-reforming fanatics. I'm sorry, but your fanatic who wants wrongs righted doesn't really interest me. He doesn't count in the evolutionary process, and my point is that evolution alone counts and man's only potential for evolution is in the life of the mind. This seems so plain and undeniable to me that it astounds me that I seem to be the only man in England today who sees it.'

He stopped, perhaps to see if anyone would rise to the challenge. I said, 'I'm sorry, but for me the very idea of "creatures of pure mind" is a repugnant one. I suppose it's a temperamental differ-ence.'

Colin shook his head. 'Call it that if you like. It seems to me, though, that Bill's right, and that you've lost your nerve, Stuart. I'm sorry. It's lonely work and I could do with some allies.' He gloomily contemplated his lonely vocation for a moment, then suddenly bounded up. He had to go, he said, to pick up Joy some-where before going on to a literary party at six o'clock. He sug-gested I should join them, saying I'd have been invited if the host had known I was in town and it should be interesting because 'Uncle Tom' (T. S. Eliot) was supposed to be going. I said I might and noted the address.

When Colin had gone I asked Tom where Carol was. Tom was surprised that I didn't know she'd left over a week before. She had moved into a flat in Bayswater with a girl she was working with. Tom gave me the address. 'But she doesn't finish work till five,' he said.

It was a quarter to four. I went to my room. Carol had left it neat and tidy and without any trace of her tenancy. There was a musty smell from the old furniture and I opened the windows to disperse it. I had been away only four or five weeks, but it was like visiting a shabby mausoleum scrupulously preserved to the memory of a dead self. There were all my books, carefully shelved and classified; there was my wall montage of press clippings, letters and pictures, my double bed, my portrait in oils done by an artist friend in Cornwall. It was all very familiar, but it all belonged to a past too close to inspire nostalgia and too distant to produce a warm glow of homecoming. The place seemed dead and inhospi-table.

Presently Bill appeared carrying two mugs of tea and full of inquisitiveness. I held him at bay for a while by asking him about the Spartacan movement. It was stuck for the moment for lack of funds, Bill told me. The Spartacan publisher had turned out to be something of a Fabian, keeping his cheque book well out of sight until he had the first volume of *Spartacan Essays* in hand. And the newspaper strike that had been going on for a month had of course meant no more publicity.

'Well now, tell me about your industrious life in the country,' Bill said. 'We've heard on the grapevine that you've been seeing a lot of Sue Rowland.'

'Quite a bit.'

Bill nodded. 'I can't say I blame you. She's a fascinating woman. Are you in love with her?'

That was a point on which I wouldn't prevaricate with anyone, except probably Carol. I said, 'Yes.'

'It's hell, isn't it?' Bill grimaced. 'I must admit I've got a touch of the old delirium myself at the moment.'

The idea of Bill being in love was somehow incongruous. 'You!' I exclaimed in amazement.

'Well, you needn't look so damned incredulous,' he said, piqued.

'But who?'

'Delphine. You met her upstairs. She's a model; top of the profession; an original mind too. But I tell you, Stuart, this love thing is a trap for the creative man. It's a delightful state to be in. Don't I know it? But it plays hell with your work.'

'Do you know it? I wonder,' I said. I suspected that Bill's confession was a stratagem for drawing me out. I didn't resent it, but I wanted him to know I saw through it.

'Do I know it?' Bill said. 'During these last weeks I've been through the whole gamut, the ecstasies of possession, the agonies of separation, the gnawing irrational jealousies. I'm an exhausted man.'

'You don't look it.'

'I mean emotionally and spiritually exhausted. That's what it does to you. I haven't done a stroke. There was nothing left to put into my work. It's no good, Stuart, we must conserve our energies. We must renounce love. Remember Kierkegaard, Kafka, Verlaine.'

Stirring clarion calls. Illustrious literary precedents. It was all as familiar and as dead to me as the room we were sitting in. I said, 'One has to live one's own life, not Kierkegaard's, Kafka's or Verlaine's.'

Bill said, 'Ultimately what every woman wants is marriage and children, and I tell you, Stuart, it's the creative man's Waterloo. Don't fall into the trap.'

I laughed. The idea of Sue laying a trap deserved only derision.

'You can laugh,' Bill said, 'but you're in mortal danger.'

'Perhaps,' I said. 'But I believe in living dangerously.'

Carol's flat was in a street of tall terraced houses parallel to Queensway on the Paddington side. A card beneath one of the bells indicated that she was on the second floor. Soon after I had pressed the bell, her voice crackled through the inter-com grille set into the wall.

'Who is it?'

'Stuart.'

'My God! Well, you'd better come up.'

The door buzzed and opened and I mounted a dim staircase. Carol was waiting for me on the second-floor landing.

'This is a surprise,' she said. It was a relief that she was neither effusively welcoming nor coldly forbidding. She seemed rather to be waiting to judge my mood. I kissed her on the cheek.

'You look well,' I said. She looked considerably plumper than a month before, particularly in the face.

'I am well,' she said, 'but I feel a mess at the moment. I've just got back from work and I wasn't expecting any visitors. Come into the flat, but close your eyes to the squalor.'

It wasn't particularly squalid. It was nondescript, like most London accommodation available for short-term tenancies, with heavy old furniture and discoloured paintwork, but the living-room was spacious and there were doors leading off into a separate kitchen and a bedroom.

'Nice place,' I said.

'It's alright. I couldn't afford it myself, but with Sheila sharing it's quite reasonable. And the coffee-bar where we work is in Queensway, so it's quite convenient.'

'Very.' We were polite strangers, awkward with each other and struggling for things to say. I felt superfluous, and that my conscientious visit was pointless. She had her life in order.

'Did you get my letter?' she said. 'I wrote to you a couple of days ago.'

'I've been away from the cottage.'

'Oh-h.' She drew it out, and her expression—elongated face, sucked-in cheeks, a slight inclination of the head—was the standard theatrical ham mime for swift mental readjustment to an unforeseen turn of events. 'That explains it,' she said.

'Explains what?'

'Your coming. I wrote to say—well, it's complicated to go into now; you'll see when you get the letter. But now you're here I suppose I'd better offer you tea.'

'Didn't you want me to come?'

'Yes and no; it depends on what your motives are.'

'Well, I wanted to see you, and to find out if there's anything I can do to help.'

'Such as?'

'I don't know. Anything.'

'I don't think there is anything. As you see, I've got my life pretty well organised for the present. Thanks for the money, by the way.'

'That's all right. I'll send you some more when I can.'

'Don't put yourself out.'

'Why not? I mean, you've been pretty drastically put out by this. It's the least I can do.'

This seemed to stir in Carol an emotion which she found difficult to control. She said, 'I'll just go and put the kettle on,' and went into the kitchen.

It was fully five minutes before she returned, carrying a tray of tea-things. Her manner declared that she had got under control whatever emotion had possessed her and was determined now to be gay and inscrutable.

'Yes, it's turned out rather well,' she said, putting the tray down on a low table in front of the couch on which I was sitting. 'Sheila's a marvellous person to share with, and she's terribly excited about the baby. The way she talks about it and makes plans, you'd think that she was the one that was going to have it. It's *mar*vellous for my morale. I'm into my fifth month now. They say it's the time you feel at your best, and it's true; a month or two ago I'd never have dreamed I could feel so well as this. I was feeling really low before you went down to the country, and I'm afraid I dragged you down with me, you poor man! I'm sorry.'

'You needn't be. It's a relief to me to see you so well.'

'Bill and Tom were very kind,' Carol said as she poured the tea, 'but I felt it was an embarrassment for them to have a pregnant woman about. It's such a bachelor establishment. I began to feel out of place, particularly in that room with all your things around.' She laughed. 'I got odd urges to change the curtains and paint the walls. It must be a sort of nest-making instinct. And also I got so tired of all that interminable talk. It suddenly seemed so unimportant. I'm sure it's me, and it's all terribly important really, but you see why I couldn't go on living there? But for Sheila, I think I'd have felt like crawling into a hole far away from anybody and just waiting for the whole business to be over. Pregnancy brings about such extraordinary changes, not only in your body but in your thinking and the way you see things. I can understand people going temporarily insane while they're pregnant. I could have done, living in that house. Isn't it the Indian Brahmins who send their women back to their mothers to go through their pregnancy and confinement? It's probably the best way. A woman needs other women at such a time, and once they've done their bit men are quite irrelevant. Bill and Tom were the soul of sweetness, but I knew I embarrassed them and would do more and more as I got fatter. It's not really fair to ask men to understand. When you think of it, it's odd even for another woman to when she hasn't been through it herself. But I suppose coming from a large family helps. Sheila has six brothers and sisters.'

It was as if she was wound up and couldn't stop the flow of talk. I detected beneath the flow a hardening edge on her voice, a slight change to a shriller key. I sought words to pacify her, to conciliate her suppressed desperation, but could find none, and I was just wondering what I would do if she suddenly burst into tears when I heard a door open. Carol jumped to her feet.

'Sheila, darling! Come and join us. I've just made some tea. Come and meet Stuart.'

Sheila was a tall thin girl with short black hair artificially streaked with silver. She had sharp features and her eyes were brown like Carol's but even bigger. She was no beauty, but by dressing colourfully and using make-up boldly she had done her best to acquire by art what was denied by nature, and the effect, I thought, was a little outlandish but not unattractive.

'So *this* is Stuart?' The voice was throaty and theatrical, and the eyes were cool and appraising. 'I must admit I've been madly curious.' She thrust out an arm and flopped her hand from the wrist as if offering it to be kissed. I shook it.

'Isn't she looking marvellous? Don't you think pregnancy does wonders for a woman? I think I'll get pregnant myself when Carol's had hers, then we'll have a cosy little *ménage à quatre*. Unless of course you've come to whip her away and make a respectable woman of her.'

Carol laughed. 'Sheila, don't tease. Stuart's just come on a visit.'

'Oh, well that's all right,' Sheila said. 'Just a social call, eh? Taking tea with the ladies. Well, I'm sorry, but this particular lady has to dash. I have a date, and I must have a bath and change. I feel positively sordid.' She swept into the bedroom.

'She's quite a character,' Carol said affectionately after she had gone. 'So you see'—she waved both arms in a gesture that was perhaps intended to indicate a sweeping away of all the past— 'all's well that ends well.'

I could have left then, but I felt sorry for Carol because her friend was going out and she would be left alone, so I suggested that she should go with me to the party. At first she protested that she was tired after working all day, but she agreed that a change of scene and a couple of drinks would soon take care of that. Then she objected that she had nothing suitable to wear, but I convinced her that even if she went looking scruffy and unkempt she'd only be taken for a best-selling novelist. She was easily persuaded, and asked me to wait ten minutes while she got ready.

The party was in full swing when we got there. The taxi took us to a large Georgian house in a crescent in Kensington, and we were admitted by a uniformed maid, who directed us upstairs. There must have been about fifty people in the elegant, high-ceilinged room, and they all seemed to be talking at once. Waiters moved among them with trays of drinks, and I stopped one and took a couple of glasses for Carol and myself. We moved round the fringes of the party and finally found Colin at the other side of the room. He was deep in argument with a man I recognised as a well-known professor of philosophy, a short, saurian man with quick eyes with heavy pouches under them.

'Come and support me, Stuart,' Colin said. 'I'm trying to persuade Professor Ayer to introduce a course on Whitehead into the curriculum at his university, but he takes the view that his work is metaphysical nonsense and not worth reading.'

'Now that's naughty!' the professor admonished, wagging a finger. 'You misrepresent me. What I said was that after his collaboration with Russell on the *Principia*, Whitehead stopped doing philosophy. *Science and the Modern World* is an interesting book, but it's a contribution to the history of ideas, not to philosophy. Most of Russell's subsequent work, too, is non-philosophical. Let's be clear about this. I've no objection to a man's writing whatever he pleases, provided he doesn't call it philosophy when it palpably isn't.' The professor spoke with a light, crisp voice, rapidly, and when he had finished he beamed.

'What about *Process and Reality*?' Colin said. 'You can't claim that that isn't philosophy.'

'I've never read it,' Ayer said, still beaming.

'Well, I think that's a deplorable admission to make,' Colin said. The professor was unruffled. 'Why? For my non-professional reading I prefer French and Russian novels, and if I occasionally have a taste for a bit of poetry I prefer to take it straight and not masquerading as philosophy. But you must excuse me.'

This last was not an apology, but a signal for the termination of the discussion. A tall man with thick grey hair and distinguished features came over, apologised for the interruption and took the professor away to meet a German confrère who had been longing to meet him.

'All logical positivists ought to be shot,' Colin spat out vindictively when they had gone. 'It irks me to see a man like Ayer occupying a chair of philosophy.'

The man with grey hair returned and apologised again for taking the professor away. Colin fulminated to him about the reputation of English philosophy depending on 'the antics of a lot of performing monkeys', and when he had got that off his chest he introduced me to the editor of a literary magazine.

'You should get Stuart to write something for you,' Colin said, and then turned away to talk to someone who had just approached him.

'I enjoyed your last book,' the editor said. 'Pity you didn't let me see a proof. I should have liked to publish an extract before it came out.'

'I'll bear that in mind next time,' I said.

'Tell me, Stuart, are you homosexual or heterosexual?' He might have been asking if I preferred coffee or tea. The tone was conversational, the corners of the mouth lifted just a little in the ghost of a smile.

I was caught off-guard and utterly discomposed. I answered, 'Well, er . . . normal, I suppose.'

'You mean heterosexual,' he said in a voice that was flinty with disapproval.

'Well, yes,' I agreed, feeling a warm flush suffuse my cheeks. That's me written off, I thought.

But I was wrong. Some time later he returned and asked if I would like to meet Mr Eliot. The elderly poet and his young wife had recently arrived and were sitting on a low couch holding hands. They both expressed pleasure and recognition when we were introduced, for I had concluded my first book with a chapter on Eliot's poetry, which, he had said in a letter, he found 'acute' and 'eminently fair and understanding', and we had subsequently corresponded a bit. But this was the first time we had met. He looked frail and he coughed a lot during our conversation, but his eyes expressed kindliness and interest. He was amused and, I think, pleased to learn that among ourselves we referred to him as 'Uncle Tom', for no doubt, being fundamentally a shy and modest man, he found the affection of the young more gratifying than their awe and reverence. He complimented me on my book on modern poetry, which he had read, and when I mentioned that my second book *Flight and Pursuit*, had been an autobiography of ideas, he said that he would never venture to write an autobiography. He thought that the exposed public position of contemporary young writers was dangerous, for it was difficult for talent fully to develop under such conditions, and he hadn't much faith in literary groups. I explained that the 'angry young man' tag that had been stuck on all young writers who had published in the last couple of years didn't really define a coherent group, though Colin, Bill and I did have a certain affinity in that we believed in the propagation of religious values. Did he not agree, I asked, that a writer should command as wide attention as possible in a time of crisis like the present if he felt he had something positive to say? But Uncle Tom wouldn't be drawn. He said, 'I think work done in collaboration is much less likely to have permanent value than work one does alone.' Then our host interrupted and introduced somebody who started to talk to the great man about the Marx brothers.

I think Eliot must have been relieved to talk about the Marx brothers after being interrogated by an earnest young world-betterer. Afterwards I felt I had made a fool of myself by falling back into a role that I no longer seriously believed in anyway.

Carol thought it was touching, the way Eliot sat holding his wife's hand, publicly declaring his love. I told her that when he was our age he had almost been ruined by a disastrous marriage to a neurotic. She took that as a veiled reference to our situation and I had to assure her that I didn't intend it as such.

When we left the party, Carol didn't want to go back to the house with Bill and the others. It was a warm evening and still light, so we walked up Exhibition Road and across Hyde Park. We walked side by side in silence for a long way. I racked my brain for chatty small talk, but anything I thought of would only draw attention to the gaping chasm between us by trying pathetically to bridge it. I felt tense and knotted inside, and kept thinking of walks in the country with Sue, which had been so gay and carefree and now seemed so irretrievably past, though the last of them had been only a few days ago.

At last she broke the silence. 'If you want to go and join Bill and Tom and the others, don't let me stop you.'

'I'll see you home first,' I said.

She laughed. 'Don't you think that's a rather unnecessary touch of gallantry in the circumstances?'

'It's the least I can do.'

'That's a favourite expression of yours, isn't it? Perhaps one day you'll try doing the most you can do for a change. That will be a day to remember.'

I said, 'I realise I've behaved despicably towards you and I deserve to be regarded as a bastard.'

She stopped walking, turned and looked me in the eyes. 'That's one of the most unkind things you could say to me,' she said.

I couldn't see it. She was intense and moved by emotions that I couldn't comprehend.

'Do you think it helps me any to be on the receiving end of your pity and your charity?' she said.

'Oh, for Christ's sake! It's not that,' I said. But as I said it I remembered Sue's 'Be kind to her.'

'It is,' she insisted, 'and it's humiliating.'

Tears came to her eyes. I took her elbow and started her walking again. Her steps were measured and deliberate. 'That you're content to have me regard you as a bastard is the unkindest cut of all. Don't you see that? You *expect* me to be the wronged woman nursing her resentment and hatred, you *expect* me to be all wrapped up in my little tragedy. You don't give me credit for any other feelings, you imagine that all the guilt and the pity are on your side. You feel rotten about the mess you've made of my life, but it doesn't occur to you that I might also feel guilty as hell about what I've done to you.'

These words, which Carol spoke in a low voice and without raising her head, produced in me a feeling of having totally lost my grip on the situation. My predominant feeling was of dismay, for I saw that the future was not going to be simply a matter of doing right by Carol in order to get off on the right foot with Sue. Carol was going to figure much larger in the situation than such a glib estimate of it allowed for. Exactly how she would figure in it I couldn't begin to predict; but the fact that she now stood revealed as a person and not a mere figure representing a wrong to be atoned for, and that she was capable of complex and to me inscrutable emotions which would have to be taken into account, put quite a different complexion on the whole situation. All this flashed through my mind as she finished speaking, but none of it came out in my reply. I said:

'But I do think that for you to feel guilty about me is putting a bit of a fine point on it. After all, you are the one who's pregnant, who's got to go through all the discomfort and pain, and who's finally going to be saddled with the child.'

'But don't you see, none of that is bad?' she said. 'I'm happy to be having your baby, I really am. The experience isn't going to damage me. I can come out the other side a better and stronger and probably happier person. But what about you?'

'I'll come out all right,' I said. I didn't entirely trust this turnabout. The positive note was just a bit too strident, the buoyancy

122

too emphatic. I didn't think that she was playacting or doubt that every word was in earnest, but I suspected that among the mass of conflicting attitudes and emotions she had temporarily fixed on and enlarged those of brave independence and magnanimous concern.

'But will you? Will you come out all right?'

'Yes,' I said firmly.

'You're so shut in on yourself. I can't begin to guess what goes on in your mind. I was quite prepared to go through with all this without ever seeing you again. I was content to regard you as the loser in the whole affair and to leave it at that. But now . . . well, seeing you makes it different. I feel . . .'

'Sorry for me?' I suggested.

'Not exactly, but sorry that you apparently aren't going to gain anything from the experience. And, poor man'—she gave a little laugh—'you're paying dearly for it, so you're entitled to gain something.' She became wistfully reflective. 'It must be a wonderful thing to go through with someone you love and who loves you.'

'Yes, I suppose so,' I said. We walked on in silence, came to and crossed the Bayswater Road and turned into Queensway. Carol pointed out the place where she worked, a glorified coffee-bar with chianti bottles in raffia baskets strung across the big plate-glass window. I suggested that we should go in for a meal, but she didn't want to. We reached her front door and I was glad when she said, 'I'd rather you didn't come up if you don't mind. When you get back to the cottage, you'll get my letter. It still applies.'

I told her I was no longer at the cottage and gave her my new address. She showed no curiosity about the change.

The next day Colin and I were alone together for a while and he asked, 'How's the Carol business working out?'

I told him she was going through with it and I was doing what I could to help.

Colin shook his head. 'Damnable business,' he laconically sympathised.

'It'll work out,' I said.

Then he said, 'Why don't you marry her?'

I was staggered. This seemed downright treachery. 'I thought you didn't like her,' I said feebly.

'I wouldn't be marrying her, would I?' he said. 'No, the way I see it, Stuart, is that one has to have a woman, and it doesn't matter much who she is, provided she's suitably adoring and doesn't get under your feet. I sometimes feel that you and Bill waste too much time up here getting involved with all sorts of people and schemes and having affairs. I honestly feel that your best plan would be to get a woman, move into the country somewhere and really get stuck into work.'

'The trouble is I'm no longer in love with Carol,' I said.

Colin was unimpressed. 'I don't think it matters. As I say, one has to have a woman. The "in love" situation is always short-lived anyway. Woman is the warrior's rest, his relaxation after the battle. It's as true for the crusader of the intellect as it was for the warriors of old. And that's what we've got to be, Stuart,' he said with rising emphasis. 'We have to be intellectual crusaders. Ken Allsop calls us "the Law Givers", perhaps a bit sneeringly, but alright, let's be just that.'

The reference was to a book that Kenneth Allsop had recently published called *The Angry Decade*, in which he devoted a chapter to Colin, Bill and myself under the title, 'The Law Givers'. Allsop had written that he found our revolt against the triviality, complacency, cynicism and materialism of contemporary society praiseworthy, our basic seriousness and our declared wish to reinstate religious values right, but he judged our rejection and our dissent too sweeping and unconsidered, and thought that by allowing ourselves to be dubbed 'angries' and by naively playing up to the Press image of ourselves, we had let our teeth be drawn. His comments on my work and Colin's had been quite generous, but Bill, he had suggested, was a dangerous proto-fascist.

Colin said he was sorry if he'd been a bit abrupt the previous evening, but he was genuinely disappointed that I seemed to have lost, if not my nerve, at least my enthusiasm for our cause. We had made a breakthrough, in a comparatively short time established ourselves as a literary group that was talked about and had to be taken into account, and now was the time to consolidate, produce more work and confound our critics. What our critics said was irrelevant, anyway, because if we pushed ahead in a few years' we would be required reading in the universities, and then it would be what *we* had said that would count. I had said something about our temperamental differences, but of course there were temperamental differences and that was our strength. It wasn't a question of any one of us being a leader and the others disciples, and we should resist the efforts of the Press and critics to make out either that Bill and I had jumped on his bandwagon or that, as had been rumoured, I had given him the theme for *The Outsider*. As he saw it, the position at present was that I had the most solid and respectable reputation, he had the biggest but the most dubious and vulnerable, and Bill so far had the least solid and needed to get another book out soon. It might be a good idea if we joined forces on a book. A subject we had often talked about and that would give our ideas a point of focus but at the same time bring out our different approaches was the concept of the hero. Why didn't we put up to Gollancz the idea of a joint book, with essays of about 25,000 words from each of us, on the theme? We must go on writing, force people to take us and our work seriously. And we must, as he'd said yesterday, keep each other up to the mark creatively. We all had our faults. I was too diffident, he tended to be too intolerant and impetuous, and Bill too careless and imprecise in expressing his ideas. Working side by side, criticising each other's work, we could iron out these faults. Bill undoubtedly had genius, but he needed someone beside him all the time to force him to take trouble and to make his meaning plain. We had to bring out the best work in each other. Eliot might believe that nothing is achieved by literary groups and that a man produces his best work alone. But hadn't he submitted 'The Waste Land' to Pound and accepted his re-write of it? That was the kind of co-operation he had in mind. In a sense he was himself very much a loner. He'd always assumed that he'd end as a kind of Tolstoy figure, occasionally uttering gloomy roars from 'Mevapolanya' and distributing bits of his garments to pilgrims. But really he hated the idea. He felt there was too much of the artist in him to enjoy being a guru. He didn't want followers, because they were always a trap. But he did, as he'd said, need allies, exchange of ideas and criticism, the sense of working not entirely alone. My emotional life was my own business. Though he personally didn't take to opinionated women, it didn't really concern him whether I finally settled for Sue or Carol. What did concern him was that we should go on working and supporting each other, and that in the next two or three years we should really consolidate ourselves as a powerful literary bloc in England.

It was both an appeal and an exhortation, and I was both moved and enthused. I assured Colin that there was no question of my deserting or giving up writing, though I did feel I needed a space of time to get my life in order and revise some of my thinking. Anyway, there was a good chance that the play would be put on at the Court, and I had got this commission for the television programme. And I agreed that we should put up to Gollancz the idea of a book on the concept of the hero. I felt I needed to be out of London, as he did, but the only thing I lacked enthusiasm for was Bill's political activities. Colin said he knew what I meant, but he thought Bill was right in believing that we should extend ourselves and make an impact on as many fronts as possible, and we ought to support him if only out of loyalty.

Later that day I went to see George Devine at the Royal Court. I had met him several times before at his house on the riverside at Hammersmith, where the Royal Court 'Writers' Group' used to meet twice a month. George was keen to make the Royal Court a genuine writers' theatre, and the purpose of these meetings was to discuss current productions, future projects and technical problems of play-writing, and to bring writers into the theatre from other media. Bill had only attended one of the meetings, after which he had dismissed the group as a 'leftist coterie'. I had been to rather more, both because I wanted to learn more about the craft of theatre and because I hoped to exert some influence on the policies of the Royal Court. It was to George Devine's credit that he gave writers, even when they were relatively inexperienced and had had no works actually performed, the idea that they could exert such influence. At the meetings, however, I had usually found myself in a minority of one, for the group comprised two main factions, the social realists and the symbolic surrealists. George's attitude at these meetings tended to be catholic and conciliatory, for he didn't want to alienate any talent.

'The best definition of theatre,' he said on one occasion, 'is still "two boards and a passion". A writer must express what he feels rather than what he thinks.' I had contested this point, quoted Shaw's 'intellect is a passion' and argued that the fault of most contemporary writers for the theatre was that they distrusted thinking.

I had called my own play *Here is Freedom* because it took place in a prison and the point of it was that here the hero discovered the true freedom of self-knowledge and religious faith. George said, when I met him that afternoon, that he thought I should reconsider the title because it was perhaps a little too didactic, but he liked the two acts I'd written, found them both moving and theatrically effective, and if I could complete the third act soon he would schedule the play for production in the autumn.

I returned to Sussex that night full of zest for work.

When I got back to the bungalow I found a card lying on the mat inside the front door. The picture side showed a monstrous piece of Westphalian civic architecture, and on the back were the words: 'Just to let you know we arrived safely. This place is as dead as it looks, but John has three weeks' leave and we're off next week for a camping holiday in France. Do lots of work and make progress with your "cure". Ever, Sue.'

Evidently she had chosen to send a card because it enforced brevity. There was nothing to read between the lines, and the way she signed off was entirely noncommittal and nicely ambiguous. It could stand as an abbreviation for 'yours ever' or as an assertion that Sue would ever be Sue, which was a thing that I didn't doubt but that in the circumstances gave scant comfort.

Well, I would teach her to try to disenchant me with cool post-cards. I would write her an unashamed love letter. I sat down immediately to do so. It took over an hour, and afterwards I read it through with satisfaction, enjoying imagining the expressions that might cross Sue's face as she read it. There were parts of it that might provoke a frown of disapproval:

'No, my love, I am not yet "cured". Nor do I see any prospect of being so. But at least I am no longer a drooling, knocked-aback infatuate with starry eyes and no faculty for concentration. Take warning that I shall never forgive you for reducing me to that state of dementia during the weeks before you went to join the army.

'Were they weeks? or days, or . . . Until I think back to details it seems they could have been only hours even, or minutes. I mean that all our times together now make up one moment and that moment still burns.'

I could see her, perhaps, taking her lower lip between her teeth the way she did when my importunities discomposed her and came near to breaking through her wall of sense and principle.

The letter, I thought, would set her back a bit in her own 'cure'. I went to bed that night well satisfied with my work.

The next morning Carol's letter arrived, forwarded by Paul, who had returned to the cottage for the school holidays. Most of it was in the vein I had expected after seeing her in London. She gave her reasons for moving out of my room, enthused about her *ménage à deux* with Sheila, explained how she had become not only reconciled to but even happy about having the baby. On the subject of my part in the affair, however, she was more explicit than she had been when we met. She said she didn't want, by selfishly insisting on marriage or nothing, to deprive me of my rights or the baby of the advantage of having a father. She had sorted herself out and had decided to keep the baby whatever happened. If I wanted nothing more to do with them ('You see, I'm already thinking in the plural') she could accept that and get used to it, but she'd rather make a clean break now than later. But if I wanted to play some part, however small, in their lives, she promised me a reasonable and unemotional reception any time I felt like going up to talk about it. If she didn't hear in the next couple of weeks, she said, she would get the message.

So when I had turned up at the flat she must have thought at first that I had received the letter and had gone up immediately to talk things over. That explained a lot. And now she would still be awaiting my response. She had said of the letter, 'It still applies.'

The two weeks passed and I did nothing about it. I couldn't see what Carol expected of me. It was clearly too early to discuss which school the child should go to or which of us it should spend the holidays with, as divorced parents did, but beyond such practical issues I couldn't see what paternity could count for. Carol had written about the advantage to the child of having a father. Probably she had had in mind something about giving the child emotional security. But I failed to see how it was possible for a father to be involved in his child's life without being fairly intimately involved in the mother's. And the most telling fact of the situation was that as yet there was no child. For the present there was only Carol, and I didn't entirely trust her declaration of independence and was wary of involving myself in any way lest I should disturb the possibly precarious balance of her present life. So indecision led to inaction, and two, three, four weeks passed.

They were weeks of productive work. I wrote the third act of the play and sent it off to George Devine. There was a letter from Colin saying that Gollancz had agreed in principle to the 'Hero' book and he had made a start on his part of it, so I began thinking around the subject, making notes and reading relevant books. I had books to review, too, for now the printing strike was over I had resumed my weekly review contribution to *John O'London*'s. I worked steadily throughout the day, and in the evening sometimes went out for a walk in the country or to one of the local pubs, where I made a few casual acquaintances. Once or twice I played cricket for the village team (when I was thirteen or so my ambition had been to succeed Len Hutton as opener for Yorkshire and England). It was a quiet, productive period. But no letter came from Sue. All I received was three postcards, from Montelimar, Aix and Perpignan. None of them mentioned my letter, and the last one began, 'In case you're still at the bungalow,' as if she expected me to have left and gone about my own life by then. They seemed to be prolonging their three-week holiday in France. I wrote another eloquently passionate letter to the German address so that she would get it when she returned and know that I was still awaiting her return and was by no means 'cured'.

This was true. I thought a great deal about her and about the marvellous weeks we had spent together before she went away. But sometimes there were doubts and questions too. She had once, in those last days, asked what I wanted of her, and I hadn't been able to answer. Nor could I now. I just wanted to offer her a totally committed and enduring love. I was certain that I could do so. But had I the right to involve her in the mess that was my life? And wasn't it just possible that my feelings for her were heightened and exaggerated by a residual guilt at not having been able to feel enough for Carol? I didn't believe this was the case, but the thought was there. And I remembered Bill recommending a flight from love and citing illustrious exemplars; and there were moments when I suspected that perhaps he was right, that love could be a haven of refuge from life's intractable imperatives. I remembered Sue's saying, 'I don't want to be your escape route,' and I was resolved that she would not be, that I would give her up rather than make use of her. But the thought of giving her up, or of losing her through my own folly, struck a cold panic into me.

At the end of September another postcard of telegraphic brevity arrived: 'Returning October 5th, about midday, Sue.' Two days later I got another letter from Carol. It was the letter I had dreaded getting. Sheila had got married the previous week and gone to live in Putney, so she was on her own again. She had got the message of my deafening silence since we met and she didn't expect me to do anything, she said, but she didn't see why I should be able to take comfort in the thought that she was lying on a bed of roses when in fact she was 'bloody miserable and sometimes desperately terrified'.

It was the nearest thing, allowing for her pride, to a cry for help. I doubted that I could in fact really help, and feared that any attempt to do so now could only lead us into a thicket of tangled motions, misunderstandings, recriminations and pain. But there was no alternative. My fate and Carol's were now inseparable. I would have to do something, and soon, before Sue got back. So I phoned Carol and persuaded her to come down the following weekend.

I took a taxi to the station to meet her. She was now quite heavily pregnant and had given up any attempt to conceal the fact. She walked with her weight thrown back on her spine. But she seemed in excellent health, with a clear complexion and bright eyes, and her manner was almost gay. In the taxi she talked about Sheila's marriage. It had come as a tremendous surprise, she said, but it was the best thing that could have happened for her, and she would make a marvellous wife and mother. The husband had a well-paid job in advertising and had been a regular customer in the coffee-bar where they both worked. It had taken him weeks to work up the courage to ask Sheila to go out with him, and no one had dreamt that the only reason he had been coming in was to see her. It was all so romantic and she was so happy for Sheila's sake, though of course she was going to miss having her around. And the flat was a bit big and expensive for her to occupy alone, but then Sheila had paid her share for the next month and wouldn't hear of having it back, and with the money I had sent her she would be able to keep the flat on at least until she had had the baby, then she would have to look for something smaller and cheaper.

Carol said all this quite cheerfully. It was impossible to reconcile her manner with the desperate tone of her letter.

I had anticipated her being curious about how I came to be occupying the bungalow, and before she started asking questions I told her that it belonged to friends of Paul Rowland who were away on holiday and would be returning soon.

'What will you do then?' she asked.

'Go back to the cottage,' I said. 'Paul is back at school now and it's empty.'

I knew from the way she had asked the question and the way she nodded at my reply that she had hoped for a different answer. But the time was not yet come for an opening of hearts and minds. Carol enthused about the bungalow and the wild garden and said it must be a marvellously peaceful place to work. I told her about the work I had been doing and she listened with interest. She clearly wanted to please. Later, while I did some writing in the sitting-room, she spent a long time in the kitchen preparing a meal.

In the evening we went out for a drink. We played darts and talked to a number of people I knew casually, and throughout the evening Carol was gay and convivial. The first tentative sounding of the deeper issues that we had both been deliberately and delicately side-stepping since she arrived came as we were walking back home from the pub.

'You certainly seem to have got a new life cut out for yourself down here,' Carol said.

'Yes. It's a good place to work.'

'Why did you ask me down?'

'To give you a break,' I said.

'Ha!' It was a sharp and derisory exclamation. 'I'm sorry,' she said, 'but it does seem a rather improbable reason after weeks of silence.'

'Well, in your letter you sounded pretty desperate.'

'Oh yes, I'm desperate all right, but a couple of days' break in the country isn't going to make me any less so. It seems to me that you just wanted to get me down so that you could show me how settled and how satisfied with your life you are.'

'That wasn't the reason at all,' I said gently. I felt that it wasn't the time to go into it. There were other people about and the night was so still and silent that voices carried. Also, Carol was getting breathless with the uphill walk. We walked on in silence, but for the sound of Carol's heavy, regular breathing. I felt guilty even about the lightness of my step, but as we passed the village recreation ground I had an urge to vault the low fence, run across the football pitch and disappear into the darkness beyond, where I would seek out the cornfield, which would now have been harvested, but would still bring back poignant memories of the night of the ridiculous moon. But I did nothing so wild. I adjusted my walk to Carol's slower one and felt ill at ease with my body. There was no ridiculous moon on this night, but the stars stood out bright and clear. I thought of interstellar space and Pascal's terror of it. It was surely an academic, a mathematician's terror. There were spaces as infinite and as terrible stretched between people.

Back at the house, I reopened the conversation. 'I just couldn't ignore your letter,' I said. 'It was, wasn't it, rather a cry for help?'

'No, just a cry,' Carol said.

I would help if I knew how, I said, but she was so changeable, sometimes full of the joys of motherhood, confidently independent, and at other times, as she'd said in her letter, miserable and terrified.

'Poor Stuart,' she said, 'can't you accept that that's exactly how it is? It's quite normal, I assure you. I'm no freak. Other pregnant women go through the same ups and downs of mood. I'm not being deliberately perverse just to make things difficult for you, I promise you.'

Yes, and other women had husbands to give them moral support. Sue had said, 'Pregnancy isn't any fun, even at the best of times.' It was, I realised, unreasonable of me to expect Carol to be all of a piece, consistently happy and capable or miserable and in need of help, just to make it easy for me to decide what to do about her.

'You have to tell me what I can do to help,' I said. 'You must have had something in mind when you wrote and when you agreed to come down.'

She shook her head slowly. 'Just hope,' she said. Her eyes were full of tears. 'No schemes to spring on you. Just a rather desperate hope.'

'But for what?' I insisted.

'I can't tell you. It must come from you,' Carol said. Then she began to cry. Big tears overflowed and ran down her face. I sat rigidly in my chair, paralysed by a conflict between pity for her and reluctance to be drawn into a scene.

'You humiliate me so,' Carol sobbed. 'You probably don't mean to or even know you're doing it, but it is humiliating to be put in the position of having to ask for favours. Can't you understand that?' She looked up suddenly and flung back her hair. A look that mingled pride and appeal flashed through her tears.

'Yes, I understand that,' I said, 'and I'm sorry I put you in that position.' But what, in lieu of love, had I to offer her? I recalled her first letter, in which she had urged me to face up to being a father. I said, 'The reason I didn't reply to your letter was simply that I didn't know what to say. How does one fulfil or even acknowledge one's responsibilities to an unborn child? I didn't know, and I still don't.'

Carol shook her head vigorously. 'It's not that now. I was being brave and trying to be a modern woman when I wrote to you, but really I'm not at all brave or modern. Frankly, I'm terrified; more and more so as the time draws nearer.'

'But what is there to be frightened of? Didn't you tell me that the doctor said you're a text-book case and that everything's going normally?'

'I'm not a case, I'm *me*,' she wailed. 'And to me it's not normal. Look!' She stood up and thrust out her belly. 'Is that normal? It's alright for the doctors to say so. They never have been and never are going to be pregnant. Can you imagine what it must be like to have this happen to you? Put yourself in my place. Men and women aren't all that different. Don't imagine that because I'm a woman I have some special faculty that enables me to accept the discomfort, the ugliness, the unnaturalness of it, and to dismiss the terror of going through the actual birth. I haven't. This hasn't happened to me before and I know nothing more about it and am no better able to cope than any man. I'm frightened. It isn't the baby that needs your help and support, Stuart, it's me.'

'I'll help,' I said. 'I'll do anything you ask.'

Carol sat down again and sighed heavily. 'That's a rash promise to make,' she said.

'I mean it. I want to help.'

'Would you come and live at the flat?'

Was she serious? It wasn't put in the manner of an appeal. It was more like a rather weary inquiry, to which she knew in advance the answer would be 'no'.

'You mean in London?' I had to prevaricate.

She nodded. 'There, I've done it!' she said, becoming tearful again. 'I swore I wouldn't beg any favours and lay myself open to humiliation again, but now I have done. I'm such a fool. I shouldn't have come down in the first place. But do you think I'd ask such a thing of you if I wasn't desperate? It seems to me not a very big thing. I'm not asking you to pretend to love me, to sleep with me or anything like that, but just to be there. We needn't even talk much. You could have your own room to work in. Oh, I know you don't want to go back to London, but would it be so terrible or such a big sacrifice just for two or three months?'

'It wouldn't work,' I said.

'But why not? Only until the baby's born, that's all I ask, then you could go your own way. I wouldn't try to stop you or make any other claim on you.'

For a moment I was tempted to tell her all. I framed the words in my head: 'The reason I can't, Carol, is that I'm desperately in love with Sue Rowland. I couldn't bear to be separated from her for three months and I know that if I lived with you out of a sense of duty or pity I would treat you abominably out of sheer revenge.' But to say that would be wilfully crushing and cruel. I said, 'No, it wouldn't work. You speak as if it would be a simple, clear and practical arrangement. But it wouldn't, would it? There would be emotions involved, and all sorts of underlying tensions.'

'Oh, you're so scared of emotions,' she said. 'It's pitiful. Let's face it, you don't want to help *me*, you just want to make some gesture to satisfy your own conscience.'

'I *do* want to help you,' I said, 'but I know I wouldn't be any help to you living at the flat. Quite the opposite.'

'Is there another woman?'

It was a natural assumption to make, but the question took me be surprise. The way she said it, though, with a suggestion of a sneer, made me decide not to tell her the truth. I didn't want Sue sneered at.

'No, that's not the reason either. You just have to accept that I can't live at the flat. I can come up sometimes, and you can come and spend some days at the cottage occasionally. And I expect to be able to help with a bit more money soon. Also perhaps I can find a cheaper flat where you can live afterwards. What do you say? Aren't there lots of little ways in which I can help without going so far as to move into the flat, which I'm sure would be a big mistake?'

'What can I say? I haven't any choice, have I?' Carol said resignedly. 'Having thrown myself on your mercy, I have to accept what you hand out, even if it's a kick in the teeth.'

'It won't be,' I promised.

'We'll see,' Carol said.

6

In the final days before Sue's return I grew increasingly apprehensive. The closer the moment of our reunion came, the fainter became my memories and the more confused my thoughts of her. Her beauty and something of her character I could recover from a polyfoto of her that I had found in a drawer, but this gave me no insight into her mind, and it was her mind that I was apprehensive about. Carol was unpredictable, but at least she was so in a predictable way, a way that I could put down as feminine and emotional. But Sue, I felt, was capable of sustaining a coolly rational truculence in matters of principle; she was capable even of putting principle before passion or self-interest. She had had two months in which to have achieved her avowed intention of getting 'cured', and it was quite possible that she had succeeded, that those marvellous weeks in July had by now been pigeon-holed in her memory under the rubric 'romantic episode', and that my still being at the bungalow when she returned would only cause her embarrassment. At the height of our passion I had respected her wholeness and resolved to do nothing to break it up, but now that I was prey to doubts and uncertainties I saw her wholeness from a different angle. I failed to see what, being whole, she could possibly gain from me.

With such thoughts and apprehensions I built up a mental image of Sue that immediately clashed with the reality when, early in the afternoon of October 5th, she returned. They arrived by taxi. I heard their voices and the slamming of car doors in the lane outside and went out to meet them. It was a hot day and Sue was dressed as she had been in mid-summer, in a skirt and blouse and sandals. She was very brown and her hair had grown longer. Daphina, her mother, was nearest to the gate as I came out, so I greeted her first with a kiss on the cheek. Then Christopher toddled up to me and I had to give some attention to his latest treasure, a friction-driven toy car.

'He's grown amazingly in two months,' was the first thing I said to Sue. I must have spent hours wondering and planning what I would say at this moment.

'Yes,' she said, 'he had a wonderfully healthy holiday, dashing about the beach all day and living on bread and olives and all those marvellous French vegetables.'

I tried to greet her with a kiss on the mouth but she turned her cheek to meet my lips.

'You've shrunk,' I said.

'I have not shrunk.' She pretended to be insulted, but her eyes were laughing.

'Are you pleased to find me still here?' I kept my hands on her waist and looked into her eyes. She couldn't lie with her eyes, and there I read the answer that I wanted.

I helped them get their luggage into the bungalow. Both Sue and her mother were impressed by the tidy state the place was in. I didn't mention that Carol had cleaned it up a couple of days before.

I had packed my things in readiness to return to the cottage— there was a bus soon—but Daphina suggested I stay. 'With all this duty-free whisky we ought to have a little home-coming celebration,' she said.

'We don't want to interrupt the flow of some work of genius,' Sue said.

'I think I can afford time off to celebrate your return,' I said.

'Is it a thing to celebrate?'

'Oh yes, quite definitely.' The novel thought occurred to me that Sue might have been as apprehensive about our meeting again as I had been. Her mother was in the kitchen. I crossed the room to where Sue was standing and kissed her softly on the mouth.

'You don't want to hang about all day while we have baths and unpack and such things,' she said. 'Why don't you get settled in at the cottage, then come back for the evening? I'll cook you a meal.' She squeezed both my hands.

There was so much to rediscover. The mental image I had formed of her had been a fond caricature, insubstantial, a creation that was not really Sue but a congeries of my own hopes, fears, longings, doubts. If just once during those weeks of separation I could have heard her voice, touched her hand, looked into her eyes,

137

she would instantly have ceased to be a figure in a situation, *my* situation, and would have become what she was to me now, a unique, complex, mysterious person with whom I had a strange affinity at a depth that had nothing to do with my situation.

I turned her curiously rough palms upwards and kissed them. 'These hands,' I said, 'those eyes, that voice, those lips, that funny long nose for looking down.' A familiar nervous look came into her eyes.

'You make me feel strange,' she said. 'What about them?'

'I'd forgotten what they could do to me.'

She looked down for a moment, then quickly up again. 'I'll cook you a curry. Would you like that?'

A curry. The day at the cottage just before she went to Germany. Life knitting itself together again, like the cells and tissues of a healing wound.

I got to the bus-stop just as the bus was drawing up. Leaving my rucksack and typewriter in the luggage space under the stairs, I took a seat on the upper deck. I had not been to the cottage since the end of July, and I fondly dwelt on the familiar scenes and landmarks of the route as a forgiven Adam might have dwelt on the scenes of Eden on his first day back. The fields had been harvested and ploughed and the lush greens of summer were turning to autumnal brown and gold. I remembered my night walks along these roads.

'You make me feel strange,' she had just said. 'Strange, strange sensations,' she had murmured, in the kitchen at the bungalow all those weeks, those months ago. And there would be other times, other summers, other autumns. There was so much to rediscover, and much, much more yet to discover. We had time. We would take love easy, let it have its seasons, let it put down roots, grow at its own pace, become strong and rich.

The familiar smell of paraffin and wood-smoke met me as I entered the cottage. On the table there was a note from Paul. I had a momentary pang of guilt at making him an unwitting accomplice to the break-up of his brother's marriage.

Settling into the cottage didn't take long. I made up a bed, put my few clothes into drawers, arranged my work and books on the table in the small upstairs room where I worked, made and drank tea, washed a pair of socks, got in two buckets of water from the stream, laid a fire, and when I had done all this there were still three hours to get through before the bus was due that would take me back. I tried first to do some work, then to read, but I couldn't concentrate, and the time seemed to drag.

When at last I got back to the bungalow Sue had already put Christopher to bed and she and her mother were drinking whisky in the sitting-room. The rich, exotic smell of cooking spices permeated the place. It was odd to be back as a guest after having spent so long alone there.

Daphina did most of the talking at first. Their holiday had been full of incidents, and she took evident pleasure in recalling them. Sue and I sat on the low couch holding hands and Sue contributed the odd detail while her mother relived their adventures. A lot of her anecdotes were quite innocent, but others, I noticed, featured Sue in relation to some admirer. An officer in the Lancers had sent her a side of venison because she had happened to mention at a party that she had never tasted it. She hadn't known how to cook it, but another young officer had taken the problem in hand and organised a barbecue party for her. In France a Minister's son had serenaded her outside her tent with a guitar and had wanted to take her up in his private plane. And how many proposals of marriage had she had? Was it three or four?—including one from an heir to a peerage who was very wealthy and would make a perfect match if he hadn't got such a big nose. One could perhaps accept him if he agreed to have a plastic surgery operation. It was all very well Sue saying she wouldn't want him even if he had a perfectly normal nose, but one had to be practical in life. The sensible thing would be to have someone like his prospective Lordship as a husband and then take Stuart as a lover.

'Do you think that would be a good idea?' Sue asked me.

'I can't really see you in the role,' I said. 'I think you'd find it very difficult to live a double life.'

We had more holiday anecdotes over the meal and then went back into the sitting-room for coffee and looked at photographs. It was soon quarter past ten and my last bus was at half past. When I mentioned the fact Daphina suggested that I should stay on and spend the night in the spare room. Only I shouldn't keep Sue up too late because it would make her bog-eyed and foul-tempered in the morning and she would have to cope with Christopher.

'You're in favour,' Sue said when her mother had gone to bed. 'First Pa offers you the bungalow and now Daphina puts you up for the night.' I should beware, she said, because Daphina's next favourite game after bridge was matchmaking and she could be quite unscrupulous about it. A product of overbreeding herself, she believed that what the family needed was some new blood, a more robust strain. She had probably marked me down for Judy, Sue's youngest cousin, who was studying in America at present but would be back for Christmas. Judy was very pretty. She had a photograph somewhere. She went over to the writing-desk and looked for it in a drawer.

'Stop playing the fool, Sue,' I said. 'I've seen enough photographs. It's you I love and want.'

'I suppose you must,' she said. 'You know, when I went to Germany I was quite sure you'd be gone when I got back.'

She asked how many women I'd had at the bungalow while she was away. I told her Carol had been down for a couple of days but there had been nobody else. I had been working hard and had lived a celibate life for four months now. She found that hard to believe. I said I wouldn't have believed myself capable of it some time ago, but it was true. 'I don't want anyone else,' I said. 'There's only you.'

She said, 'I came back fully intending, if you were still here, to talk to you very severely. I had all sorts of sensible reasons and arguments lined up.'

'You think we should part?' I said.

'We shouldn't have come together. And you should have gone back to London before I returned.'

'And lived with Carol? That's what she wants. She asked me to live with her until the baby's born.'

'You should.'

'Do you want me to?'

'We're not talking about what I want. I should get my life in order too.' And when we had both got our lives in order, she said, we might find that we no longer felt the same. I might find I didn't want her any more. I said it was more likely to be the other way round. I'd come back with a nice shining clean slate, only to find that I'd lost her.

'It's a risk we both take,' she said.

I said, 'It's a risk I'm not prepared to take.'

She asked about Carol. I told her she was well, still working, seemed to be looking forward to being a mother but sometimes to be frightened at the thought of the actual birth. Sue said she remembered the time she'd had with Christopher, the depressions during her pregnancy, the sense of being completely alone, the terror of dying or of the child's dying or being malformed. 'We can't think of ourselves as the central figures in this,' she said. And, 'The trouble is, I can't be sure how I'll react over a long period in a situation that goes against the grain.'

'You mean the famous stomach might rebel?'

She smiled. 'You could put it that way. It does seem to be a rather special thing we've got. I don't know why it is. I don't really understand it at all. It's like a tender shoot that could grow into a great big tree, but is in danger of being crushed or blighted before it gets a chance.'

'We'll put a big fence round our tender shoot,' I said, 'and put "Keep Out" notices on all sides.' But that wouldn't help, she replied, because we were both inside the fence and were quite likely to tread on it by accident.

She told me that in Germany she had allowed a young officer to fall in love with her, which had been a bit unkind, but it had all been linked, she said, with her imagining my having a procession of women at the bungalow.

I said, 'I see I shall have to lock you away, if only to protect innocent and vulnerable young men.'

'I don't want to be locked away,' she said. 'The trouble with you men is that you assume the right to claim a woman body and soul. And what do you offer in return?'

I said, 'Body and soul.'

'In that order,' she said, 'and with a big gap between.'

'My love for you is without any gaps between.'

'So what do we do now?' she said.

'Muddle through.'

'To what?'

'I don't know,' I said. 'I only know I can't let you go.'

Sue was abstracted and thoughtful for a while. I had to cajole her to tell me what was on her mind. It was that Brian had written to her while she was in Germany. He didn't accept that it was all over between them. He considered that now he'd got a job and sorted himself out they ought to try again to make the marriage work.

'You must tell him,' I said.

She shook her head. 'He's coming down next week. I don't want him to get the idea that I'm leaving him for someone else.'

'Why not?'

'Because I'm not. That isn't the reason. It was over with us before you came on the scene.'

Brian had a holiday. He would stay for a few days, perhaps the whole week. 'And you want me to keep out of the way?' I asked.

'I don't want you to,' she said. 'But on the other hand I don't want him to know. You see how difficult it is, this muddling through.'

While they were away I had slept in Sue's room, but that night I slept in the neighbouring spare room. I expected to be racked with frustration after my months of celibacy and with her so close. When we kissed goodnight she said, 'Think of our tender shoot.' She left the doors of both rooms open and was soon asleep herself and I found the sound of her regular breathing and the sense of her proximity strangely quieting and didn't suffer the expected pangs. It was enough for the present to have had my anxieties allayed. The cool truculence I had feared, the sacrifice of passion to principle, had not been in evidence. She had confessed to jealousy, weakness, need, an acceptance of muddling through. In her absence I had idealised her, exaggerated her self-possession, her control, her good sense. That was certainly one aspect of her. But another was the one she had shown tonight, as a woman caught up in life, perplexed, passionate, vulnerable, nervous and apprehensive, and moreover with problems in her own life quite as difficult as mine with Carol. What if Brian should persuade her to try again to make the marriage work? It was as unthinkable as that I should marry Carol now, but unthinkable or not it was a thought, and a recurrent, nagging one. Carol's role in this whole affair was not unique; love had made more than one conquest, life claimed more than one victim.

I had to go to London later that week to look up some material at the Hulton Picture Library for the television programme. Sue came with me. Since her return we had spent every evening together, but I had managed to do some work at the cottage during the days. As we were now set in for a long period of 'muddling through', it was essential to establish and pursue some routine of work, so we had resolved not to meet in the days except at weekends. The trip to London was an exception, an opportunity to be together. From the station we phoned Tom, who invited Sue to go over while I was at the library so that I could pick her up at Chepstow Road later in the afternoon.

I got through my picture research quite quickly, so I decided to call in on Carol on my way over to Tom's. She wasn't at her flat, so I went round to the coffee-bar in Queensway. She was working in the kitchen, but as it was a quiet time of day she was able to come out, sit at a table and have a coffee with me. I thought she was looking tired and asked why she didn't pack the job in and live on the money I.had sent her. But she said she hadn't much longer to do before she qualified for maternity benefit and it would be a pity to forfeit that now.

'Well then, come down to the cottage for a few days' break next week,' I said. 'Can you get time off?'

That wasn't any problem, she said. But what was the point? Her last visit hadn't exactly been a relaxing break. I told her I thought we might spend a day or two looking for a flat for her. I had been thinking about it, and it seemed that life would be a lot easier and cheaper for her, and healthier for the baby, if she moved out of London, perhaps to Hastings or Eastbourne. Flats could be found for about a third of London prices in Hastings.

It was true that I had been thinking about it and had come to this conclusion, but of course the invitation wasn't entirely altruistic. Brian was going to be with Sue the following week.

'I'll think about it,' Carol said, meaning the proposal that she should take a seaside flat.

'Well, come down anyway,' I said. 'Come on Sunday and meanwhile think it over.'

'You're a strange man,' she said. 'Talk about me being changeable! You want something of me, but I can't make out what it is.'

'All I want is for things to turn out as best they can for you,' I said.

'There's more to it than that,' she said.

That was shrewd of her, I reflected afterwards as I walked along Westbourne Grove on my way to Tom's, to say that I wanted something of her. I hadn't thought of it that way. I had thought of her at different times as the martyr, the victim, the passive recipient of charity, the beneficiary of the overflow of my love for Sue; but that she had an active role, that she could yet give something that I needed, was a new angle on the situation. What did I want of her? Not exactly forgiveness, but something akin. An honourable release perhaps. If in my private drama she had been cast as a victim, I in hers must have been cast as the heartless tyrant, and what I wanted was to be released from this role. But how? Perhaps by letting her know about Sue, so that she would see me not as a tyrant but as a man in love. Was this selfish? I thought not. It would surely be less humiliating for her to know that I was not so much repelled by her as attracted by another. She was bound to find out sooner or later, and when she did she might well reproach me with having deceived her, having treated her with misconceived kindness when it would have been better to have given her credit for being able to face up to the whole truth. To let her know about Sue would be to give her an opportunity to play more than a passive, receiving role in the situation. And if she really was concerned about how I was going to come out of it, and felt guilty about what she had done to me, as she had claimed during our walk through Hyde Park some weeks before, then it was only fair to tell her the truth, for knowing it she would no longer have to feel guilty.

All this seemed very plausible, and I might have turned back and made my confession there and then had it not occurred to me that by doing so I would be involving Sue more than I had any right to, and it might affect her problem with Brian. The ethics of the whole business were really too bewildering.

Sue was with Tom and Bill when I got to the house. Bill greeted me with his usual manic bonhomie and immediately started sounding off about the poet Chris Logue, who had just rung up to say that he'd heard a rumour that the Spartacans had joined forces with Sir Oswald Mosley and were going to support his party's candidate in the North Kensington constituency in the forthcoming election. Logue had warned Bill that if this were true we would meet fierce opposition from the Left, and not only on the political front. Several prominent publishers and magazine editors and also the Royal Court theatre might close their doors on us. We should grow up and stop meddling in politics, he had said. Bill, of course, was furious, and his imprecations were eloquent.

I asked him how the rumour had arisen. It was true, he said, that he and Colin had met Mosley. They had had a drink with him at his house in Chelsea a couple of weeks before. Bill had found him an amiable, cultivated man. They had talked more about philosophy, literature and music than about politics. Mosley, Bill thought, was probably one of the most able and intelligent men in British politics in this century, and an example of how the mediocrities that made up the Establishment ruthlessly put down a man with talent and vision.

'I don't know if he had talent,' Tom said, 'but he certainly lacked judgement. He threw in his lot with the wrong bunch, didn't he?'

'The trouble with your generation, Tom,' Bill said, 'is that you're haunted by the great bogey-man figure of Hitler. The extermination camps were the great trauma of European experience. European man has been paralysed ever since.'

However, there was no question of the Spartacans joining forces with Mosley or helping his party in any way. Perhaps Mosley had been hoping to get some free publicity on the 'Angry Young Man' bandwagon and had played his cards shrewdly, been the friendly, cultivated host at the first meeting. But it had been, so far as Bill and Colin were concerned, merely a social call. They had accepted the invitation mainly out of curiosity. How the lefties had heard about it he didn't know, but they were now certainly showing their colours as scandal-mongers and alarmists.

I wondered if this would affect my chances of getting my play on at the Royal Court. I hadn't yet heard anything from George Devine, except for an acknowledgement of receipt of the third act. 'We must get our own theatre,' Bill said. He was writing a play called *The Titans*, but he wouldn't let the Royal Court have it if they begged him.

He had a message for me from Colin. If I didn't write to him he would in future refrain from signing his letters to me so that I wouldn't be able to sell them for a vast sum in twenty years' time, and when he went on his lecture tour in the States he would spread rumours that I was given to sodomy and bestiality. He had already completed his contribution to our proposed 'Hero' book, but it had run over length and Gollancz had suggested that he should publish it as a separate book under the title *The Stature of Man* and consider my contribution and Bill's for separate publication when they were completed.

The most shattering news I learnt on this visit, however, was that our landlord, Les, had been killed in a car crash. His wife was going to sell the house and we had all been given three months' notice. None of us had known Les particularly well, but we all had reason to be grateful to him, for he had enabled us to live cheaply for a couple of years. He had once accepted a worthless picture from me in lieu of a month's rent. Of course, he did well enough out of the girls in the basement and on the ground floor, and it was good policy for him to be easy on us as a landlord because he knew he could rely on us to preserve his incognito. Once when two official-looking men came to the door inquiring who the owner of the house was and where he lived, Bill told them he was a little mid-European fellow called Franz Kafka and sent them to an address in Muswell Hill. But now poor Les had paid the wages of sin and his wife was going to cash the business in and go and live in Malta. So I would have to find somewhere to put all my books.

Sue and I got an early evening train back to Battle. During the journey she told me that before I had arrived at the house Bill had given her a lecture on the demanding and responsible role of the woman in a writer's life. Love, he had told her, is a trap for the creative man. A writer needed a docile, background woman, one who made few demands on life for herself and was content to be an appendage, a martyr to the man's work. He didn't think she was cut out for such a role, and he could only see two possible outcomes of our relationship: either my work would suffer or I would give her a hell of a life. She had told Bill that she didn't think it was a matter that concerned him and it was an incredible impertinence to speak like that, but what he had said had sunk in and it echoed some of her own private doubts and worries. She could never settle for being an appendage, she said. When she had separated from Brian she had resolved that in future she would live her own life, in her own world.

'I want *our* life, *our* world,' I said.

But what would that be like? she asked. I couldn't answer that.

146

We'd see. And what about the great works? Perhaps Bill was right, and it was deprivation, frustration and desperation that brought out the best.

I said the great works would take care of themselves. They'd find their way out in time if they were there. But would they? she said. They might not. They might have to be forced out. It was a thought.

It was a cliché, this image of the artist as martyr, as the great sufferer, the self-denier. But was there not, I wondered, an element of truth in it? 'What have we to do with happiness? We have a duty to our genius.' Bill's was a dramatic view of life, but it was possible that to hold and act on a dramatic view was the only alternative to making of life an undistingiushed compromise, or to succumbing to all the complexities and perplexities and being merely a myopic minion of the force of circumstances. There were other and more authoritative advocates of the dramatic point of view. There was Yeats:

> 'The intellect of man is forced to choose
> Perfection of the life or of the work,
> And if it take the second must refuse
> A heavenly mansion, raging in the dark.'

There spoke a man who should know, who had gone on evolving, as man and poet, through a lifetime. Sue shared, I knew, my fundamental belief that life is growth, that there is no compromising with life's imperative: evolve or perish. She wouldn't put it like that, perhaps, but the way she lived and thought implied such a view. And what had I to contribute to her growth? There was another imponderable. Bill was right to stress that the pursuit of happiness was not man's highest aspiration, and if love conferred only happiness, and not growth, it must be ephemeral. But to renounce love, I felt, would be to renounce life, and so to preclude growth. I felt sure that Sue believed this too, for now she had this kind of fatalistic acceptance of the situation. But, like me, she doubted, wondered and was perplexed.

When I told her that I had invited Carol down for the week when Brian would be with her, she confessed to mixed feelings. Of course I was right to ask her down, she said, but she didn't exactly relish the idea now of my having another woman at the cottage. I asked her how she thought I would feel, knowing her husband was with her all the time and that he wanted to get her back. We'd have to act, pretend, suffer in silence. Might it not be better for everyone concerned if we simply told them the truth? But Sue didn't agree, and I promised to be discreet.

I had a shock when I met Carol at the station, for she had suddenly turned blond. She looked rather shamefaced about it.

'Don't say anything,' she said, 'I know it looks horrible.'

'It doesn't,' I said, 'but why did you do it?'

'God knows. I felt so dowdy. I suppose it was pregnancy blues. I got fed up with being myself. And all I succeeded in doing was making myself conspicuous and horrible. I feel everyone's looking at me.'

'Well, you'll be able to relax at the cottage,' I said. 'There'll be nobody to look at you there.'

'Except you,' she said. 'And of course you don't count, since you find me horrible anyway. You needn't deny it. It's a fact I've learnt to live with.'

When we arrived at the cottage she cooed over it. 'It's the sort of place I could settle for,' she said. 'A hideaway, a hole to crawl into, that's what I want. Shall I move in? Shall I write a letter giving my notice and just stay on here?'

She put the suggestion teasingly. Since she had got off the train she had been in this peculiar mood, superficially gay and animated, but with bitterness showing through. I asked her what the hell had got into her.

'Oh, I'm fed up to the eyeballs with being the good little martyr that everyone tramples over,' she said. 'I've decided from now on to be myself.'

'If that means being embittered I think you'd do better as a martyr,' I said.

'*You* think!' she said. 'Oh yes, it's much more comfortable for you if I bravely suffer in silence. But I'm not concerned with making it comfortable for you; not any more. From now on it's me that counts. You've stood by me, as I suppose you'd call it, in such a lame and half-hearted sort of way. Am I supposed to be grateful? Are you really so godlike that to be admitted into the Presence once in a while should count as such a great favour? I'm inclined to believe that that's how you see yourself, because no other explanation of your behaviour makes any sense.'

Of course, there was an explanation that made very good sense, and again I was strongly disposed to tell her everything, but I said nothing, and she probably interpreted my silence as further evidence of my magisterial indifference.

'You're so insufferably smug,' she said. 'I thought you wanted something of me, that that was why you kept up this half-cock relationship. But I don't think you need anything from anybody.'

'You're so wrong,' I said.

'Did I catch a note of real feeling?' she said. 'Well, if you want anything from me you'd better spell it out because I'm no good at guessing games. And if you don't, if all you want is to square things with your own conscience, then you'll have to put up with all my moods and tantrums and demands, won't you? Or else of course throw me out. But as long as you keep me around, or keep on extending the helping hand of charity to the poor maiden in distress, I shall be myself and say and do exactly what I want.'

These were fighting words and they seemed to announce a real change in her attitudes and conduct. But rage did not come easily to Carol, and when it did come it was soon dissipated. During her stay she busied herself about the cottage quite happily on the days when I worked. She cooked, cleaned, went shopping, took long walks from which she returned with bags full of late blackberries and sometimes hazel-nuts. We spent two days flat-hunting in Eastbourne and Hastings. She agreed that it might be a good idea to move out of London when the baby was born, but on these trips we didn't find a flat that appealed to her. I said I would buy the local papers and keep looking during the coming weeks.

One afternoon I was sitting upstairs at my work table in front of one of the windows when I saw a car pull up on the grass verge beside the road and three people get out. Carol was blackberrying in the middle field between the cottage and the road and couldn't see the visitors at first because of the high hedgerows. Not until they were approaching the middle field could I make out quite clearly that the woman with the two men was Sue. I watched as the two women in my life greeted each other and walked down towards the cottage together with the two men behind. Afterwards

Sue told me that Carol was so friendly, welcoming and unsuspecting that it made her feel terribly guilty.

One of the men was Brian, and the other I recognised as a character who frequented the local pubs and whom Sue had spoken to sometimes. He was a short man with a handlebar moustache, an affected voice and the unlikely name of Peregrine, and I had taken an instant dislike to him which had been in no way mitigated by his bar-side bonhomie and generosity in dispensing whiskies.

When I went down to meet them Brian apologised for the intrusion and said he had just come to pick up one or two things Paul had asked him to take back to London. Perry had been so good as to drive them over from Battle.

Sue hadn't been able to object to their coming or to accompanying them, she told me later, because it might have aroused Brian's suspicions. When I greeted her with a kiss on the cheek I felt her stiffen, as if she feared that I would wrap her in my arms and give everything away. I invited them to stay for a cup of tea. We sat around in the garden.

'Many a happy hour I've spent out here, bashing away at the old typewriter,' Brian said. He talked about the time, fifteen or twenty years ago, when he and Paul had lived at the cottage together. He addressed most of this to Perry, which gave me an opportunity to watch Sue, who, however, avoided my eyes. Carol was in the cottage preparing the tea.

'So how are you getting on with the problems of the universe, Stuart?' Brian suddenly said. I said I thought they were yielding gradually to patience and steady work, and I looked at Sue and tried to make it a message for her.

'I read your last book,' Brian said. 'Remarkable stuff for a man of your age. Mind you, there are things in it that I would quarrel with.'

'There are things in it that I quarrel with,' I said. 'I wrote it over a year ago, and there have been some fundamental changes since then.' Her eyes said, Message received, but please, stop it.

'Of course, one's ideas change and develop all the time,' Brian said. 'And books are so final; I think it's a brave man who commits himself to print on any question of a philosophical nature.'

'I don't know.' I said, 'I think there comes a point when you have to commit yourself and face the consequences, when you've to say, "Here I stand; I cannot do otherwise." ' I was enjoying this game of recklessly declaring my love to Sue while apparently talking quite seriously to her husband. But this time she didn't look up.

We had tea, chatted, laughed at some of Brian's stories. Carol was relaxed, exuberant, enjoying the change. Sue was quiet, withdrawn, hating every moment of it, and soon after tea she said she had to get back because of Christopher.

'Didn't she use to come to Chepstow Road with the man in the white Vauxhall?' Carol said when they had left.

'James. Yes, that's right,' I said.

'I got the impression that she and her husband were separated,' she said.

'Perhaps they've got back together.' I immediately regretted saying it. In the atmosphere the last hour had engendered, being secretive and covering up had become a sort of game, and I was still playing it.

'They didn't look very together,' Carol said. 'She sat there as if she was thoroughly bored.'

'Perhaps she's heard all his stories before,' I said. 'Marriage to a raconteur must be rather boring after the first careless rapture— if ever there was one, which I think extremely unlikely in their case.'

Carol raised an eyebrow. It was one of the subtler of her theatrical 'takes'. I had slipped up, shown a sharpness that was out of character. I didn't know what she would make of it, whether she would see through to the jealousy and resentment or put it down as a lapse from my accustomed godlike imperturbability, but I knew she noticed it.

There was one encouraging development during this week, a letter from George Devine saying that the Royal Court would like to put on my play, which I had re-titled *The Tenth Chance*, as one of their Sunday evening 'Productions without Decor'. Also I managed to complete the script for my television programme, a job that I found particularly difficult going. The programme was supposed to be an illustrated essay explaining why my generation rejected political and religious orthodoxies. Photographs and clips from newsreels were to be used to give a graphic visual background to the text, which I would read. The idea was to show that because we had been repeatedly disillusioned by our elders' failure to match their actions to their ideals, and because we had the great threat of nuclear annihilation hanging over us, our generation, and the articulate angry section of it particularly, felt that the old orthodoxies, party politics and the religion of the churches, were no longer relevant to our condition. I could argue the case well enough. It had a grain of truth in it, but it was only a partial truth, even for me, and whether it was true for my generation as a whole I had no idea. The last war, the bomb, our elders' failures, were problems that had been very remote from my life and thought during recent months, and I would feel something of a fraud sitting before the television cameras pretending that these had been the great formative influences on my life. Sue had meant more to me than Stalin, Chamberlain, Hitler and all the other monsters or martinets of modern history, but I could hardly put that to an audience of millions as a statement representative of the views of my generation.

So I had no enthusiasm for the work. But the BBC had paid half my fee in advance and spent money on filming and gathering material, so I had to complete it, and I reckoned the best time to do so was this week. On the Friday I worked throughout the day and evening and broke off only to go down to light a fire for Carol to sit by and get in some logs, then later to eat the supper that she cooked. Carol didn't object to my absorption in my work. She sat all evening in front of the log fire, knitting and reading St Exupéry's *Flight to Arras*. When I went down about eleven o'clock she looked up from the book and smiled.

'Done a good day's work?' she said.

'I don't know about good,' I said, 'but I've finished the wretched thing.' I sat in the armchair at the other side of the fire and looked through my manuscript.

Carol said, 'Good,' and went on knitting. I thought, What a cosy, domestic scene: the woman, in full bloom of pregnancy, happily knitting and at the same time improving her mind; the man, just returned from an exhausting foray in the realm of ideas to the comforts of hearth and home! It's the common, the consecrated pattern, and perhaps it's folly to demand more of life.

'Do you think you're a representative woman of your generation?' I asked her.

She laughed. 'What a funny question. Why?'

I said that as I was supposed to be speaking for our generation I'd welcome her reaction, at least to the ending of my piece, which I read out to her:

'We believe we are attending at the birth of a new world, and we express our faith in it by saying No to the old. No! to the specious freedom that is offered us on a plate. No! to the big empty words, political slogans and rallying-calls. No! to tyranny. No! to hypocrisy. No! to prejudice. No! to fear. And No! to all the vast, impersonal things that make men feel insignificant beside them. And it is at this point that our No becomes a Yes. It becomes an affirmation of our belief in man's power to change his world. It becomes an assertion of our independence; yes, of our freedom. So at the last moment we discover that we have a cause to fight for. We cannot fight for it on the barricades. Its battles must be fought in the loneliness of our own minds and hearts. But nonetheless the cause is the same cause as all the great wars and revolutions in history have been fought in the name of: the cause of freedom. Freedom today begins in understanding. We can't score for freedom by putting a cross on a ballot paper or joining a Church. We serve it best by standing outside the clash of ideologies, interests and factions, and promoting among people an understanding of themselves and their world. If this understanding makes them say No to the present order of things, we are prepared to face the consequences of this. And with this No on our lips we will endure, steadily working towards the light and patiently waiting for the dawn of a new era.'

'Well, would you say that that has the authentic ring of the voice of our generation?' I asked Carol.

'I don't know,' she said. 'It certainly has a ring.'

'You mean that to you it's just me making noises?' I said. 'Well, you're right. But that's what the television people want.'

'I think it will go down very well,' Carol said.

I laughed. The theatrical term was apt. 'Yes, it will go down,' I said, 'though not in history; into oblivion rather, but at least I'll get paid for it.'

Sue had had a harrowing week. There were signs of strain and nervous tension around her eyes and mouth. She was on tranquillisers. It wasn't that Brian had been difficult or unreasonable, she said. He had wanted her and Chris to go and live with him in London, but had finally come round to accepting that there was no future for them together. He had even agreed to give her grounds for divorce. But it had been an ordeal for her, having to persuade him, and discussing the question of what part he was going to play in Christopher's upbringing. Christopher had been difficult all week too, fractious and tending to hang on to her skirts all the time. He had picked up the atmosphere of tension and anxiety. And she had missed me and wondered what was happening with Carol. She was worn out, she said, and she felt she must look a mess.

I said, 'You're beautiful and I love you.'

'You're certainly seeing me at my worst,' she said.

I told her about my week, Carol's moods, our vain flat-hunting, the acceptance of the play, my work. I gave her the television script to read, and told her I wasn't happy with it because I felt that it wasn't really me.

'Do you mean you don't believe it?' she said.

It wasn't exactly that, I said. It was that this level of yea-saying and nay-saying wasn't the level on which real life was lived. It didn't touch on anything fundamental. Life was much more complex and difficult and the really vital issues were not so clearly polarised. Besides, it wasn't new.

'Does a thing have to be new to be worth saying?' she said.

No, I said, but it should be deeply and personally felt. The problem was to find one's own voice. I had a certain facility with language, but eloquence was not thought and a feeling for words could conceal a lack of feeling for anything else.

She didn't say anything, but I guessed that she was thinking about Bill's warnings, perhaps his 'Love is a trap for the creative man.' So I said, 'It's my being in love with you that has made the difference, but in the long run that can't but have a good effect.'

'What about in the short run?' she said. 'I shouldn't like your friends to say that it's been the ruin of you, that there goes another man fallen a casualty in the war of the sexes.'

'I don't care what they say,' I said.

'But I do,' she said.

It was soon after this, after the week when Brian and Carol had been down, that we made love for the first time. Sue came with me to the cottage one evening. I had bought half a bottle of brandy. We both needed it to steady our nerves. We sat in front of the fire and drank half of it. It was a cold evening, but it wasn't the cold that made my teeth chatter. When I led her up the narrow, dark wooden staircase her hand squeezed mine in little convulsions. She whispered that she was very inexperienced and I said I would love her tenderly and gently, and afterwards she said:

'I have much, much more to give you.'

'We have years, my love,' I said. 'We'll develop and explore it through a lifetime.'

And it was extraordinary to say a thing like that and really believe it.

7

I found a flat that I thought would be ideal for Carol. It was in Hastings Old Town, and comprised the second and third floors of a tall terrace house on the East Hill overlooking the harbour. Away from the seafront, with its monuments to the banality of human wishes—amusement arcades and makeshift wooden huts that offered summer trippers beach teas, fortune-telling, souvenirs, comic postcards, shell-fish and ice cream—the old part of Hastings had charm and dignity. There were low, oak-beamed houses, winding streets, surprising passages opening into courtyards, terraces, pavements elevated above street level. I thought it wouldn't be a bad place to live and work.

The flat was spacious and from the windows of the main room there was a magnificent view over rooftops with varied elevations down to the harbour and the sea. The rent was reasonable and the kindly old landlady, who lived below, had no objections to having an unmarried mother and her child as tenants.

Carol came down the first Saturday in November to see the flat. She liked it and got on well with the landlady, so I paid a month's rent in advance.

'The place does rather need redecorating, though,' Carol said.

I was so relieved that she had agreed to take the flat that I said I would redecorate it myself before she moved in. Decorating wasn't the kind of work I relished or had any aptitude for, and I felt afterwards that my promise had been rash, but I reconciled myself to the work by thinking of it as a penance that would win me a degree of absolution.

That Saturday was Battle Bonfire Night. Battle Bonfire is a famous annual event in Sussex, a carnival occasion with big bands, a fancy-dress procession, a splendid pyrotechnics display and an immense bonfire on the 'Green', which is in fact a concrete car-park in front of the medieval Abbey. Carol had seen a poster advertising the event and said she would like to see some of it before getting a train back to London. This was awkward because she had originally said that she would get an early train back and I had arranged to take Sue out that evening. When I tried to discourage Carol by pointing out that we had a long wait before eight o'clock, when the festivities began, she said, 'Why don't we call on your friends Brian and Susan? They live in Battle, don't they?'

I phoned Sue and explained what had happened. She said she supposed it would be alright if we went over for tea, but we would have to be careful and discreet.

We were very discreet. We managed to get away together briefly in the kitchen, where I told Sue about the flat and kissed her and told her that things were working out, but the rest of the time we spent all together in the sitting-room. Daphina told stories about her life in India, to which Carol listened and responded with interest. Then when Sue put Christopher to bed, Daphina asked Carol about her pregnancy and the arrangements for her confinement. I thought what a strange woman she was. By now she knew about the whole situation, but not once had she expressed an opinion about it or shown any disapproval of my involvement with Sue. And she didn't seem to feel that having Carol in the house put her in an awkward position. She was neither cool nor excessively solicitous towards her. With Sue's approval she sorted out and gave to Carol a carrier-bag full of baby clothes, saying, 'My dear, they grow out of them so quickly, it's only practical to pass them on to someone else.'

The meeting seemed so painless and uncomplicated that I saw no reason why we shouldn't all three go out to see the bonfire festivities. When I suggested it I could see from Sue's expression that she didn't want to come with us, but this time I disregarded the wisdom of the gut and pressed her to come. Daphina supported me, said she would be quite happy to baby-sit, and finally Sue agreed to come though I could tell that she was still reluctant.

It was about a ten-minute walk to the Green. I walked between Sue and Carol, linking both their arms and holding Sue's hand in her pocket. We could hear the military band in the distance as soon as we left the bungalow. Sue called on her social training to meet the awkwardness of the situation, and chatted about the local bonfire night tradition. For centuries the district had been noted for the manufacture of high-quality gunpowder and up to three or four years ago the home-made firework called the 'Battle rouser' had been one of the hazards of bonfire night, but its use had now been forbidden by the police. Even so, one had to have eyes in the back of one's head because there was always a crowd of youths who came for the fun of letting off bangers and jumping-jacks in the crowd. It was best to stand with one's back to a wall. But we ought to get near to see the actual lighting of the fire, which was always done with a royal flourish by Mrs Harboard, the eccentric lady whose family had owned the great estates of the area for centuries and who still behaved as if she were a kind of viceroy.

Carol walked on, looking steadily ahead, without making any sound or gesture to acknowledge that she was listening to what Sue was saying. The stiffness of her arm and the set of her face showed that she was completely absorbed in her own thoughts and feelings. I thought, Yes, she must have guessed. Hell, this isn't how it should have happened.

Sue, too, picked up the atmosphere and finally gave up being bright and informative. She looked up at me as we walked and her eyes were troubled and said, This is a big mistake. I felt utterly miserable. I thought, This isn't the sort of situation Sue should have to cope with. I've been stupid and insensitive. I wondered if she would ever forgive me.

When we got to the top of the High Street the procession was just beginning. It was led by a military band. Behind the band a disorderly crowd of people in various historical costumes danced and clowned, and the rear was brought up by a phalanx of black-robed and hooded figures carrying long flaming torches. We joined the crowd moving along the pavement beside the procession. It was not possible to walk three abreast. There was a lot of shouting and cheering and people rushing to catch up with the band jostled past. Occasionally a firework was let off. Pieces of flaming rag dropped from some of the torches and were kicked into the gutter where they lay smouldering. Mindful of Carol's condition, I tried to stay beside her while Sue walked on a little ahead.

'It's a bit hectic,' I said. 'Are you going to be alright?'

Carol said, 'Yes, I'm quite used to being pushed around.'

We were able to get together again at the Green, where we walked around the enormous bonfire, as yet unlit. On the top, silhouetted against the night sky, was the figure of the guy tied to an old chair. I wondered if Carol was wishing Sue up there in its place.

A lot of people had accompanied the procession to the other end of the village, where it would turn round and return in about ten minutes for the ceremony of the lighting of the fire, but others had remained in small groups on the Green. The two high towers of the Norman gateway to the Abbey loomed over the scene, and Sue pointed out the little door in the arched wooden gates through which Mrs Harboard would presently sweep to put the first torch to the fire. Again Carol pointedly ignored her. I tried to elicit from Sue a look to signal that all would be well with us when this ordeal was over, but her eyes only met mine briefly and they were expressionless.

We stood around in silence, watching the crowd, getting well clear of occasional fireworks, while the sound of the returning military band got louder. When the procession returned to the Green the torch-bearers formed a three-quarter circle round the bonfire. The music stopped and the crowd became hushed with expectancy.

Sue suddenly said, 'Look, there's Malcolm Frazer and his crowd. I must go and have a word with them.' And before I could say anything she had left us. I watched her thread through the crowd to a group of young people, who greeted her warmly. I recognised Malcolm Frazer as the plummy-voiced City type who had driven Sue home from the cottage one night in the summer.

A cheer went up when Mrs Harboard, dressed in a black cloak and wearing a broad-brimmed black hat, appeared in the Abbey gateway holding a blazing torch at arm's length. She made her way to the bonfire with a long, slow stride like a dancer's and paused dramatically before plunging her torch into the tinder. Then she stepped back to allow the torch-bearers to make a circle around the fire, whereupon they moved in and all at once hurled their torches onto the pile.

Carol said, 'It's like being back in the Middle Ages. You can imagine what it must have been like to be present at a witch-burning.'

There was a lot of movement in the crowd and people were laughing and shouting and more fireworks were going off. I couldn't see Sue anywhere. I said, 'Let's walk around a bit,' hoping to find her. But Carol took no notice.

'Oh, look!' she said, as enormous Catherine-wheels started spinning on the towers of the Abbey gatehouse. Then there were rockets, Roman candles, more Catherine-wheels. 'But this is the best place to see the display from,' Carol said when I suggested again that we should walk around.

The display took about twenty minutes. When it was over Carol said, 'What happened to your friend?'

'She went to have a word with someone she knew,' I said. 'She's probably lost us by now.'

'We've been in the same place all the time,' Carol rightly observed. Then after a pause: 'Well, if you're so worried go and look for her.' I was about to say that perhaps I would when she added, 'But I won't be here when you come back.'

'Oh, come on, Carol,' I protested, 'don't be so unreasonable.'

'Unreasonable! Ha! I like that! He expects me to be all pally with his new mistress and he tells *me* not to be unreasonable.'

'Sue is not my mistress,' I said. I felt that it wasn't exactly a lie. We had only been to bed together two or three times, and all in the last two weeks, and anyway she was much more to me than merely a mistress.

'Then why did you lie to me about her husband?' Carol said. 'On the day they came down to the cottage you said that perhaps they were back together, when you must have known they weren't. I suspected it then from the way you looked at her.'

A firework exploded a few feet away from us, making Carol jump. I suggested we went into a pub to talk.

'What is there to talk about?' she said. 'You might as well put me on a train to London then go and find your Sue and make it up to her. I suppose she'll forgive you. Everybody always has done. That's your trouble.'

But she came into the pub and we found a corner table. When I returned from the bar with our drinks and sat down she said, 'Why did you insist on her coming when she obviously didn't want to? For the satisfaction of having both your women in tow at the same time?'

'No, that wasn't the reason,' I said.

'Why then? To humiliate me? I'm well aware that in this condition I can't offer any competition to an attractive woman like Sue. You didn't have to rub it in.'

'I didn't intend that,' I said. 'I may be stupid and insensitive, but I'm not malicious, and the last thing I want to do is to hurt you unnecessarily.'

'Poor man!' Carol said. 'You must have gone through agonies deciding just how much hurt was "necessary". But I can't really sympathise. It's a problem I wouldn't mind having.'

She meant it, she said, about wanting to get back to London. She didn't want to get back too late and she certainly didn't want to have to spend the night at the cottage. So we left the pub, walked across the Green, round the great bonfire and then out of the circle of its glow into the darkness. It was about a five-minute downhill walk to the station.

'I want you to know,' I said as we walked, 'that Sue has all along urged me to do everything possible for you. She's even tried to persuade me to go back to you.'

'Great for her,' Carol said, unmoved.

I said, 'I'm telling you that nobody has been callous and calculating or taking pleasure in putting you down or deceiving you, as you seem to imagine. Neither Sue nor I particularly wanted to fall in love, not in this way, not so seriously at this time. But it happened. We found that we were stuck with it, and with each other.'

'Oh, I see, it's a case of "this thing is bigger than both of us".' She ham-acted it.

'If you want to reduce it to a cliché, yes.'

'It is a cliché,' Carol burst out. 'This whole bloody mess is a cliché, and I'm sick of it. Do you expect me to be impressed that you fancy you've found your great love? It's happened before. And even if it is different this time, what's that to me? I'm going to be stuck away in a flat with a baby.'

Yes, I thought, my agonies of conscience can never be commensurate with the day-to-day suffering and loneliness that I've put Carol through and committed her to for a long time to come.

At the station we learned that we had twenty minutes to wait for the next train to London. We went into the Railway Hotel to get out of the chill night air. It was crowded and noisy and there was nowhere to sit. We had to push our way through to the bar.

While I was getting the drinks, Carol said in a low voice, 'She's over there.' I felt a surge of relief, but though I looked all around the bar I couldn't see Sue. 'In the other bar,' Carol said. The public bar had a separate entrance and was partitioned off from the saloon, but the partition stopped at the bar. I saw Sue standing against the far wall with a group of people among whom I recognised Malcolm Frazer. I also recognised another member of the group, John Woodley, a man of about forty who dressed like a teen-ager, in tight trousers and leather jerkin, and lived in a cottage in a neighbouring village. His features were slack and leery, and I didn't like him being anywhere near Sue, but at least Malcolm Frazer was between them.

'Why don't you go to her?' Carol said.

'I'll see you on the train first.'

'Or we can both go round. Then you and Sue can come and put me on the train, wave goodbye and live happily ever after.' She was smiling, in a way enjoying it, but she couldn't hide the hurt. It was in her eyes.

I said, 'I hope you're not always going to be embittered about this.'

'It's possible,' she said quite gaily, 'but it's not going to be your worry, is it?'

I kept an eye on the group in the other bar, but didn't attempt to attract Sue's attention. We had a couple of drinks then I took Carol back to the station. The train was on time. Just before she got on to it, Carol said, 'You should read that book *Flight to Arras*. Towards the end there's a passage where he says, "To create love, we must begin by sacrifice." That struck me as very true. But I don't believe that you're capable of sacrifice. That's why I don't believe in this great love of yours for Sue.'

'You'll see,' I said. But I thought, What have I to sacrifice?

When I got back to the Railway Hotel the group was just leaving the public bar and crossing the car-park. I was some distance behind them when I saw John Woodley, who was beside Sue at the rear of the group, suddenly put his arm round her shoulder and bend down towards her. She tried to twist away and I heard her say, 'No!'

I had about twenty yards to cover and by the time I got there John Woodley had heard me coming, turned round and crouched down, ready for me. I had alerted him by calling out, 'Don't you dare touch her, you lousy bastard!' Woodley's face was amused and vicious. Crouching, weaving his body, arms held at the ready down by his knees, the palms of his hands turned towards me, the fingers beckoning all at once, he said, 'Come on, come, come on then.' My idea of a fight was a standing-up, man-to-man exchange of blows, and Woodley's stance discomposed me. Nevertheless I flailed in and tried to land a blow on his face, but before I could get near enough I was doubled up by a kick in the crutch, which was followed by a rain of sharp blows on my head and face. I went down. I felt dizzy and the pain was so acute that I couldn't straighten out. People around were shouting. I heard Woodley's voice saying, 'Fuck me if I know what it's all about.' Sue was kneeling beside me on the ground. She said, 'Are you alright? Oh, you shouldn't have done that. He fights dirty.' The pain diminished and I was able to get to my feet again. I said, 'I could kill him. If I had a weapon I'd kill the degenerate slob.' And I meant it, with my whole being and without any reservations. In a cool part of my brain I knew in that moment that I was capable of murder. I was shaking all over and, inexplicably, tears had come into my eyes, but as the pain ebbed new energies surged into my limbs and I was keyed up to launch myself at Woodley again. But Sue was hanging onto me and Malcolm Frazer and two other young men were between us, remonstrating with Woodley and trying to hustle him away. Sue said, 'Stuart, for my sake, please! He didn't do anything.' I said, 'He didn't get a chance, did he? But what if I hadn't been here?' The thought of how accidental my presence had been, and of what might have happened to Sue if I hadn't been there, started me trembling uncontrollably again and brought the stinging tears back. I broke free of her and rushed towards the group surrounding Woodley, but I couldn't get at him. There were more people around now, and some of them grabbed my arms and held me back. Woodley, among a group a few yards away, was laughing and saying, 'I'm prepared to forget it. In fact I admire a man who stands up for his woman.' Someone said, 'There, you see, why don't you shake on that and make it up?' I said, 'An evil, degenerate slob like that shouldn't be walking about. I just want to kill him. Why do you all interfere?' A voice said, 'He'd kill you, mate.' Then Malcolm Frazer and Sue hustled me back into the bar while some of the others made sure that Woodley got off the scene.

Malcolm Frazer bought me a large brandy which I took in a trembling hand and gulped down. He said in his plummy voice, 'I do agree with you about Woodley. He's an unmitigated swine. I'm only sorry you didn't manage to lay one on him.'

Sue took my hand and it stopped trembling. Her grip was tense and her eyes anxious. She said, 'I'm sorry, but I had to leave you. I couldn't bear seeing Carol so hurt and humiliated.' When she asked where Carol was and I said she had gone back to London she was concerned and said I shouldn't have let her go. I had to convince her that Carol had meant to go back anyway and that it was perhaps better now that she knew the truth and we didn't have to be secretive and deceitful. I had shown myself an insensitive idiot this evening and I was sorry for having put both of them in an intolerable situation, but it would blow over and on the whole things were looking better now that I'd found a flat that Carol liked and was going to get it ready for when she had had the baby. Sue looked doubtful that it was going to be that easy.

Malcolm Frazer, who had been talking to someone else meanwhile, turned to us and invited us to go with him to a party that friends of his were giving in Robertsbridge. Sue said she had to get back home early because of Christopher, but thanked him for the invitation and for his help, and I offered him a drink before he left but he said they had to be going and to keep it till next time.

I suggested that we should have our own party at the cottage, and Sue should stay the night. We hadn't yet spent a whole night together and experienced the relaxed intimacies of the morning after a night of love, and we both longed to. But she couldn't, she said, ask her mother to cope with Christopher in the morning at such short notice, and although Daphina was probably fully aware of the nature of our relationship it wasn't really fair to put her in a position where she had to admit the fact and to condone it. I wasn't going to argue with her about another principle involving someone else's feelings after this evening's blunder, so I took her home and caught the last bus out to the cottage.

I didn't get to sleep easily that night. My mental camera kept re-running the events of the evening, particularly the abortive fight. I re-scripted the scenario and saw Woodley beaten, bleeding, begging for mercy, or dead. Strange, this nostalgia for violence. I puzzled over Carol's parting words, the quotation from St Exupéry,

'To create love, we must begin by sacrifice.' That might apply to love of a country or a cause, or to a mother's love for her child, but I didn't see that it necessarily applied to mature human sexual love. I had sacrificed nothing to win Sue's love. For me it had been all gain. But love, I myself had said, is an opportunity, and yes, I would welcome an opportunity to make a sacrifice for Sue; not in order to create love, for it was already created, but to express it. As I had expressed it in my attack on John Woodley. It was an extraordinary, intoxicating, liberating feeling, to know oneself capable of murder. *There* was the link between love and sacrifice. Love was not born of sacrifice, nor was it a reward bestowed upon the good, the selfless, the compassionate. Really to love was to know oneself capable of giving or taking life for the loved one's sake. And though compassion would say, 'Bestow your love where it is most needed', Life said, 'Love is not yours to bestow. It lays claim to you.'

Sacrifice, self-giving, violence, love, anguish, desperation: suddenly these had become realities, no longer just concepts to juggle with or mere bricks that had to be built into a philosophy before it could plausibly call itself 'existentialist'.

I went to London for some of the rehearsals of my play at the Royal Court. George Devine had appointed Anthony Creighton, co-author with John Osborne of the play *Epitaph for George Dillon*, to direct my play. He and the cast were enthusiastic about the work, and the first rehearsals went well.

'You should hold out for a full-scale production,' said ever-militant Bill. 'It's a scandal that these mediocrities take such a damned patronising attitude to genius.' But there was no question of a full-scale production at this stage. If the Sunday production went well, George Devine said, they would then consider bringing the play into the repertory. I signed a contract under which I got £15 and the English Stage Company had an option on my next two plays.

Colin was delighted. 'This could be our breakthrough,' he said. 'The Royal Court is, after all, the only serious theatre in the country at present, and I think we ought to use it at least until we can set up our own theatre.' Bill didn't agree. He thought I was selling myself cheap.

George Devine had reservations about the last act of the play, the greater part of which was taken up by a dream-sequence in which the hero, who at the end of the second act had broken down under interrogation and betrayed his comrades in the Resistance, underwent a series of harrowing experiences of terror and rejection before finding peace and fortitude in religious faith. The jump from the realism of the first two acts to the fantasy dream-sequence of the third, he thought, would present a problem for the director, and he would be interested to see how Tony Creighton dealt with it. The whole point of the play, I emphasised, was that the first two acts were dominated by external action and conflicts, but in the third act it became a 'drama of inwardness'. If the audience were still watching a play by the time we reached the dream-sequence, it would probably fall flat. They should rather be participating in an experience, undergoing a sequence of emotions rather than watching a sequence of events. We had to use every technical device possible to involve the audience totally. Tony Creighton suggested that we should play the dream-sequence scene against a musical background, and together we chose part of a movement from a Bruckner symphony as appropriate to the mood of the scene.

At the Writers' Group meetings I had sometimes argued with George Devine about Shaw. 'The theatre must be a place of liberation,' George said. 'Didacticism and discussionism on the stage are oppressive.' I said I didn't think Shaw was oppressive, but Beckett was, with his world- and life-weariness and his dreary symbolism. This was in reference to the Beckett play, *Endgame*, which George had himself recently produced at the Royal Court. George considered Beckett to be a dramatist of the first rank, and I had argued with him that a man with such a negative and despairing view of life must be a second-rater. Shaw, I maintained, was the great master of our craft, and the Shavian theatre should be our model.

The Tenth Chance, however, was more influenced by Sartre and Eliot than by Shaw. Sartre's influence stemmed from his definition of freedom as 'total responsibility in total solitude', and was also in my choice of hero, a Resistance leader imprisoned by the Nazis in an occupied country. The influence of Eliot was in the theme, the qnest for religious faith; and in writing the final scene of the play, which was ritualistic and incantatory, I had in mind the ending of Eliot's *The Family Reunion*.

The theatre was full on the night of the performance. I sat at the back, surrounded by friends. Colin and Joy had come up for the occasion, Michael and Anne Hastings were there, and of course Bill and Tom. Only Sue was missing. She had insisted that I should take Carol.

The first two acts went splendidly. The audience was hushed and attentive and seemed to be gripped by the drama and the argument. I received a lot of compliments in the intervals and was encouraged to think that George would have to transfer the play into the regular repertory. Then the third act started. I knew instantly that our decision to accompany the dream-sequence with music was wrong. The dramatic tension was lost and I could sense that the audience was no longer held together in its response. Near the end of the act a woman in the stalls—we later learned it was Elaine Dundy, Kenneth Tynan's wife—got up and left the theatre noisily. Then in the climactic scene a voice called out loudly, 'Rubbish!' Colin shouted from the back of the theatre, 'Shut up, Christopher Logue,' and Logue also made a noisy exit. When the curtain came down there was an outburst and the audience split into factions, boos and catcalls vying with applause and cheers.

The newspapers made much of the ensuing scene in the pub next to the theatre. 'The Angry Young Men Get Angry With Each Other' one of them gleefully announced. 'Sloane Square Stomp' trumpeted *Time Magazine*, whose article slyly mocked everybody involved. 'Stuart Holroyd Starts a Storm in the Theatre' said *The Stage*. I wasn't present at the scene that caused all the furore. It happened before I went into the pub. By all accounts, Colin, Bill and Michael Hastings were involved in a scene with Logue and Tynan. Colin was reported to have said, 'We'll get you. We'll stamp you out, Tynan,' and 'Tell your friend to keep his filthy mouth closed in future.' To which Tynan replied, 'Stay out of my life, Wilson,' and said to onlookers, 'There's your supposed leader, you're younger generation. He's a dictator.' Then there was a scuffle in the course of which Logue landed on the floor. One report had it that he had been dragged down by the hair by Colin, and another that Michael had pulled his chair from under him. When I went into the pub I was steered away from the corner where all the action was by Sandy Wilson. 'Keep out of this, Stuart,' he said, and led me to the bar where John Osborne, dissociating himself from the factions, said, 'Terrific! It looks as though the English theatre's waking up at last.'

Bill said later, back at the house, 'It's the best thing that could have happened. You'll get national coverage tomorrow.' And he was right. The story made the front page of the *Express* and the *Chronicle* and all the other papers carried some mention of the incident. Bill was jubilant. 'This is what we've needed all along, a news story that clearly polarises the two camps among the Angries. From now on it's out-and-out war.'

In the afternoon I received a telephoned invitation to confront Chris Logue on the television programme, 'Tonight'. Bill was full of advice as to how I should 'demolish' him. However, I didn't feel any personal animosity towards Logue, nor, I think, did he towards me. Our confrontation in front of the cameras only lasted about five minutes. Logue started by arguing that the theatre ought not to be a place of genteel entertainment and decorous behaviour, but a platform for debate and argument, and if a man found a play's argument objectionable he had a right, even a duty, to say so. The interviewer asked him what he had found objectionable in the play. 'Its sadism and its bogus Christianity,' Logue answered. 'The idea that one can find God by undergoing torture seems to me deplorable, and I object to the idea, implied in every line of the play, that we must suffer, that attempts to check, alter, reform, change our suffering are impudence.'

I replied that nothing of the sort was implied in the play, that it didn't celebrate torture or suffering and it certainly didn't exonerate the torturers. It made a statement that torture is a fact of political life and that a man with the will and the seriousness to do so could grow through the experience instead of being destroyed by it. It wasn't a play about social reform, it was about religious experience. Someone had mentioned the word 'fascistic' in connection with it. Well, it seemed to me more fascistic, doctrinaire and repressive to hold that the word 'God' couldn't be used on the stage except as a mild expletive.

In such television confrontations as this, the interviewer can favour one contestant by giving him the last word. Whether it was by design or accident I never knew, but our interviewer called a halt abruptly after my little speech, leaving Logue feeling thwarted and piqued.

'This publicity is enough to fill the theatre for a month at least,' Bill said afterwards. 'If Devine doesn't put the play into the repertory now he'll be showing where his true allegiances lie.'

When I phoned Sue and told her I would return to Sussex the next day she tried to dissuade me. Surely there must be lots of exciting things happening, she said. I was a national celebrity. Shouldn't I remain in the thick of the fray? I said there was no fray. To the newspapers we were just good copy and for the television people we were cut-price performers. If there were going to be any battles of ideas and principles fought they wouldn't be fought through the media.

Bill said I was chickening out, there could be all kinds of developments in the next few days. I said I had work to do and couldn't just hang around and wait for developments.

'You should make things develop,' Bill said. 'Go to Devine, demand a full-scale production and tell him you'll withdraw their option on the next play if he doesn't give you one.'

'I'll write to him from the country,' I said.

I did write to him in fact, but not in the tone that Bill suggested. To my inquiry whether, in view of all the publicity, there was any chance of the play going into the repertory, Devine replied that unfortunately the programme was full for the next two months and after that two key members of the cast would no longer be available. It had been a pleasure and an honour to put on my play and he hoped it wouldn't be long before he saw my next one. Incidentally, did I know that Sir Oswald Mosley had been in the audience on Sunday and, rumour had it, was going to write a review of the play in his magazine, *The European*?

I didn't know, but I could imagine the glee with which the Logue/Tynan faction would seize upon the news. I was well out of it. Literature should be concerned with simple, profound, eternal things, not with the ideological twitterings of freaks and fanatics.

The work I had told Bill I had to do in the country was not literary. Carol's time was drawing near and I had the flat to get ready. I bought some second-hand furniture and carpets and a gas-cooker and gradually got the place reasonably habitable. I slept there some nights so that I could get on with the decorating early the following day. Sometimes Sue came down and helped, but progress was much slower than I had anticipated. There were vast areas to paint. I hired a Rediffusion radio and television input. Carol wouldn't be able to get out much with the baby and would need some entertainment, and I could relieve the tedium of the work to some extent by listening to music while I did it. The work went slowly and my money went alarmingly quickly, and I hadn't quite finished when, one morning, Sue came down and told me that Carol's friend Sheila had phoned, as arranged, to give the message that Carol had gone into labour and was in Charing Cross Hospital.

When I phoned the hospital at midday there was no news. She was still in the labour ward. They suggested I should phone at intervals of about four hours. Sue said I should go to London so that I could visit Carol in the evening if she had delivered by then, and spend the night at Chepstow Road. And I should ring her in Battle as soon as I had any news. So I took an afternoon train to Charing Cross and called in at the hospital as soon as I arrived. Still no news. It was an unusually long labour, they said, but there was no cause for alarm and I could phone for news now as often as I wished.

When I got to Chepstow Road Bill immediately took me into his workroom to show me his latest brainwave. He had got a sculptor friend to make a blue plaque similar to those that the London County Council fixed to buildings to announce that famous people had lived there. Bill's plaque announced: John Braine, Tom Greenwell, Stuart Holroyd, Bill Hopkins, Colin Wilson lived here 1956–1959. He had arranged to have it firmly fixed to the front of the house the following week, just before they moved out. He had looked into the legal aspect and found that there was no law against such self-advertisement, probably because it had never occurred to the official mind that anyone would ever have the audacity to do it. There was going to be a ceremonial unveiling and there would be photographs and reports in the papers.

Tom thought it was a splendid stunt and an appropriate cock-a-snook ending to the 'angry decade'. It had been a good time, and it was sad to be splitting up and going our separate ways. Still, we would always be welcome at his new place, a big flat situated below a nonconformist church in Kensington. That too, he thought, was oddly appropriate. He would put up a notice with arrows to direct callers. It would read: Heaven's Above and Lucifer's Below.

Bill had found a flat in Paddington. He said he would take my books and other belongings with him and store them until I needed them. But what was I going to do now? He'd heard I'd got a nice flat for Carol. Wouldn't it make sense to move in with her and get stuck in to work? I said I hadn't decided where I'd live yet, but it couldn't be with Carol.

When I rang the hospital again late that night I learned that Carol had just had a boy and they were both doing well. I would be able to visit them in the morning. I phoned Sue to give her the news and to arrange to meet her the following afternoon in Battle.

I hadn't seen Carol since the night when I put her on the train, though I had spoken to her once or twice on the phone to consult her about how she wanted the flat decorated. I couldn't imagine how she would feel now and when I went to the hospital in the morning I was apprehensive and prepared for anything. I went armed with flowers and fruit. A nurse showed me into a ward of about thirty beds and pointed out Carol's in the far corner. She was lying face downwards and didn't see me enter. There were no other visitors at that hour and I felt embarrassed crossing the ward bearing the traditional offerings. A group of women were playing cards at a table in the middle of the ward and others were in their beds, reading, knitting, chatting to their neighbours, or sleeping. They all watched me and I felt like an intruder.

When I appeared beside her, Carol turned over and sat up. I kissed her on the cheek. She smiled and her eyes shone. That was a relief. I said she looked well.

'I feel marvellous,' she said. 'You can't imagine what a luxury it is to be able to lie on your stomach.' She had had a bad time, a lot of pain, but it was over now and it had been worth it. The baby was perfect, and so sweet, such a blind helpless thing with little wavy arms. I should see him, but I couldn't at present because they took them away between feeds to let the mothers get some rest.

'I'm so glad I went through with it,' she said. 'We did the right thing, didn't we?' I said I didn't know about the 'we'. She was the one who had gone through all the suffering. 'No,' she said, 'you

171

went through it too, but in a different way. And I promise that we won't be a burden to you.'

She looked radiant and lovely and I wondered whether, if I hadn't met Sue. . . . But I suppressed the thought. I told her about the flat, described how I had decorated it and the furniture I had put in. She would be out of hospital, she said, in five days' time, and I said I would be able to finish the work by then. I would come up to bring her out of the hospital and help her settle in.

I told her about Bill and Tom and she laughed at the story of the blue plaque. Not until I was about to leave did she mention Sue. 'I hope you'll both be happy and make something worthwhile,' she said. 'Will you get married?' I said yes, Sue and I probably would get married in due course, but she would have to get a divorce first and that would take time. I tried to put it gently, so as not to hurt, to convey in my voice and manner that this was not a matter of choice but of destiny. But now there were tears in Carol's eyes. 'It does seem ironical, doesn't it,' she said, 'that you are going to be father to another man's child?' She didn't add, 'When you won't have anything to do with your own,' but it was implied.

I said, 'I know.' To say what was in my mind, that I hoped one day she would find someone, as Sue and I had found each other, would sound heartless and complacent.

When I left the hospital I went straight across to Charing Cross station and took a train to Battle. I had arranged to meet Sue for tea in the Pilgrim's Rest, next to the Abbey. It was not the kind of place we went into normally, but I had suggested it because at this time of the year we could be sure of privacy there. It was an olde-worlde tea-house, a large barn of a place with high ceilings, oak beams, carefully laid tables with lace doilies, and elderly shuffling waitresses.

Sue was already there when I arrived, sitting at a table in a corner. There were signs, by now familiar to me, of stress and anxiety around her eyes and mouth.

'How's Carol?' was the first thing she said.

I told her that Carol and the baby were both well, that Carol was now glad that she had gone through with it, and about the arrangements I had made to bring them down to settle in to the flat the following week.

172

'Are you sure you don't want . . .?' she began, and I had to urge her to go on and say what was in her mind. 'Well, now you've got a son you might feel differently,' she said. 'You might want to go and live with them.'

'I shall never feel differently,' I said. 'I've told you before, I want our world, our life. I want us to marry and be together always.'

Her eyes searched mine and in hers I could read questions: is it desperation? a way of escape? an emotional reaction? And I tried to tell her with my eyes that it was none of these.

'Months ago we promised to protect each other from getting married again,' she said.

'I know,' I said, 'but this is the only way we can stop each other getting *wrongly* married again.'

Sue said, 'I have Christopher.' I said yes, and I'd be a father to him, and we'd have other children and love and live and grow together through a lifetime. I said that now I couldn't conceive of life without her.

'But what about your work?' she said. 'Perhaps your friends are right. Perhaps you shouldn't marry.'

I said that I didn't believe that a writer must renounce love and marriage for the sake of his work, that that was a romantic notion and I wasn't that kind of romantic. Perhaps I used to be, but a lot had changed in the past months. Now I put life first and work second, and I believed that ultimately the work could only benefit from putting them in that order. And one day, I hoped, I might even be able to write about love.

'One day I might,' she repeated. 'Brian used to say that.'

'Are you comparing us?' I said.

'No, I was thinking about myself. I shouldn't like to be the type of woman who destroys ambition in a man.'

She was so serious. I laughed. 'You couldn't destroy anything,' I said. 'You're a giver of life.'

I believed this with all my heart and all my intelligence, but I did not, I could not possibly in that moment foresee what her gift of life and love would entail for me in the years to come. I who had always been the chooser, the maker of my own life, and who delighted now in a sense of being the chosen, in being tossed into the current of life and borne along by it, could not then foresee the

173

humility, the dissolution of the sense of the unique importance of self, the loss of ambition and of the arrogance perhaps necessary for creative work, the seductive satisfaction of just serving and caring, that love, happiness, and ultimately fatherhood, would bring. Still less could I foresee the long, hauling effort it would take, one day, to recover self and soul, to summon memory, intellect, feeling and imagination to the task of making coherent that time when I had simultaneously lost and found myself.

DATE DUE